Finding and paying for
residential and nursing home care

Carers Handbook Series

Finding and paying for residential and nursing home care

Marina Lewycka

BOOKS

© 1994 Marina Lewycka
Published by Age Concern England
1268 London Road
London SW16 4ER

First published 1994 in Age Concern Books' *Caring in a Crisis* series
This edition published 1998

Editor Caroline Hartnell
Production Vinnette Marshall
Designed and typeset by GreenGate Publishing Services, Tonbridge, Kent
Printed in Great Britain by Bell & Bain Ltd, Glasgow

A catalogue record for this book is available from the British Library.

ISBN 0-86242-261-2

Bulk orders

Age Concern England is pleased to offer customised editions of all its titles to UK
companies, institutions or other organisations wishing to make a bulk purchase.
For further information, please contact the Publishing Department at the address
above. Tel: 0181-679 8000. Fax: 0181-679 6069. E-mail: addisom@ace.org.uk.

Contents

About the author

Marina Lewycka is a lecturer and freelance writer. She contributed to the BBC handbook *Who Cares Now?* and her training resource pack *Survival Skills for Carers* is published by the National Extension College with support from the Department of Health. She has been involved in the organisation of weekend courses for carers. She is also the author of the first book in this series, *The Carer's Handbook: What to do and who to turn to.*

Acknowledgements

This book is the product of many people's ideas, experiences and expertise. I would like to thank all those who were willing to share personal and often painful experiences, as well as some happy ones. They have given the book a human dimension which sets the factual information in its context, and will help others in a similar situation to make their difficult choices and decisions.

At the same time, I would like to thank all those at Age Concern whose expert knowledge and involvement have made the book much more accurate and readable than I could have done alone. I would like to acknowledge Sarah Butler, David Moncrieff and Marion Peat for their practical support, Evelyn McEwen, Barbara Meredith, Sally West, Audrey King, Lorna Easterbrook and Jane Whelan for their expert comments, Vinnette Marshall for painstaking work on the copy, and Caroline Hartnell for doing so much more than an editor usually does.

I would also like to thank the people in Leeds and Sheffield housing and social services departments, especially Bronwen Holden, Stephanie James, Robert MacDonald and Christine Rose; Dorothy White of the Relatives Association, and Bruce Sparrow of the British Federation of Care Home Proprietors, who answered all my awkward questions so helpfully.

Finally I would like to thank Jenny Williams, Josie Midgley and all the residents of Headingley Hall, who made me so welcome and from whom I learned so much.

Introduction

The need to move into a care home can come about suddenly, through a crisis such as illness or bereavement, or it can develop over time. Either way, it often brings about a crisis in the family, and decisions may be made in a hurry or under pressure. It is easy, in this situation, to make a wrong decision, or to worry afterwards that the decision was the wrong one.

Nevertheless, there are many excellent care homes out there, where older people may enjoy a better quality of life than they would struggling on at home. This book aims to help them.

Deciding on residential or nursing home care is never easy, either for the person involved or for their family. For the older person it means accepting that one is no longer able to manage on one's own. Life in a care home may seem to represent the end of independence and the loss of dignity. Harder still, it means accepting that one's own family is not able to provide the care that is needed.

For the family, this is often a time of guilt and anxiety, of feeling they have 'let their relative down'. The relatives of an older person who needs to go into a care home can feel isolated and without support. They may feel under pressure – from friends or other members of the family, or from health and social services professionals – to act in a way that seems wrong both to them and to their relative. The usual sources of help and support may therefore seem to have turned against them or vanished.

This book guides the reader through the decision-making process, and looks at some of the alternatives to going into a care home, for example staying in one's own home with additional support or moving into sheltered housing. It explains the differences between residential homes, nursing homes and dual-registered homes and suggests things to look out for and questions to ask to satisfy yourself that the home you choose is a good one. It also looks at the financial implications, both for the person going into a care home and for their family. Finally, it discusses what you can do if there are problems with the home you and your relative have chosen.

This book is written for the family or friends of anyone who needs to go into a care home. People already permanently in a care home before April 1993 are covered by different financial regulations. For more information about these see Age Concern England Factsheet 11 *Financial support for people in residential and nursing homes prior to 1 April 1993.*

The book refers to the person going into a care home as your 'relative' – and it is perhaps most likely to be one of your parents, or a spouse or partner. But it could be a grandparent, an uncle or aunt, a brother or sister, or a close friend. The information is also relevant to older people looking at the options for themselves. The person who needs to go into a care home is referred to as 'she' throughout the book because it is more usual for older women to find themselves in this position. But of course the information is equally relevant to older men.

It is hoped that where possible the family and the person needing care will discuss all the alternatives together, and reach a decision that works for everyone.

1 Deciding to move into a care home

The decision to move into a care home can be one of the hardest decisions a person ever has to make. Although it can – and should – be a positive decision, for too many older people it seems to represent the end of independent life and dignity. For the relations of an older person, too, this is a difficult decision. People often say they 'couldn't live with themselves' if they 'put Mum or Dad into a home'. Yet in some cases this may be the best or the only practical option.

If you have to make the decision on behalf of someone who is not mentally capable of deciding for herself, it can be even harder to be sure you are doing the right thing.

This chapter looks at how best to make the decision. It looks at some of the issues you and your relative might want to consider, and explains how the social services department will assess your relative's need for care. Finally, it looks at your feelings and those of others concerned.

Jean

'Then the social worker said, "Who are you keeping her at home for – for her, or for you?"'

'For eight years I had been caring for my mother, who had Alzheimer's disease. I went over to her house every day to look after her. At the same time,

1

I was still running my own household as well as working full-time. My daughter was getting up an hour early in order to call in on her way to work. My husband helped out too. In fact all the family pulled together. I was determined that we would look after her. After all, she was my mother, and I hated the thought of putting her in a home. It was a battle at first to get anything from social services. The local Age Concern were very helpful – they told me what I should ask for and who I should contact, and they offered her a place in their day centre.'

Someone from social services came round each morning to help Jean's mother get up. The evening was covered by the family, with help from Age Concern. A charitable fund paid for Crossroads Care attendants for six hours a week. She was able to go to the Age Concern day centre twice a week and the council-run day centre four times a week. But in the end even this level of care was not enough.

'One day she fell and broke her wrist. The hospital plastered it up and she was discharged. We explained that she had Alzheimer's, but they insisted on trying to show her how to do physiotherapy exercises. She couldn't even understand why she had a plaster on her wrist. We coped as best we could, but it was a nightmare.

'This was when the social worker told me she really needed to go into a care home. But when a vacancy came up and we visited the home, we didn't like it at all. It was a big home, and Mum would have had to share a room. I just couldn't come to terms with it, so I turned the place down.'

Jean turned down two more offers of places without even telling her family. She didn't want them to pressure her into accepting.

'I knew that once she went into a home she would never come out. And I just couldn't do it. Then another place came up at a new residential home, and we went down to look at it. We both liked it, but I still had my doubts. Then the social worker said, "Who are you keeping her at home for – for her, or for you?" So I agreed. I cried my eyes out, but it seemed the only thing to do.

'People may think it's taking the easy way out, to put your parents into a home. But for me it wasn't easy, it was unbearable. It was the hardest decision I ever made.'

It took Jean's mother a while to settle down in the home, and Jean felt anxious and guilty.

'She used to say, "Have you come to take me home?" It's only recently that she's realised that it is her home. Now when she comes to my house, after a while she says, "I want to go home." Now that I know she's properly cared for, I have peace of mind.'

Taking time to reach a decision

The need to move into a care home may develop gradually, over a considerable period of time. It may also be a crisis, such as an accident or a sudden illness, that forces you to face up to the question of residential or nursing home care. You suddenly realise that someone who seemed to be coping well on her own can no longer do so. Or it may be that the death or illness of someone who lived with her has left your relative vulnerable and alone.

In this situation, you and your relative may feel under great pressure to make a decision in a hurry. This is definitely the wrong thing to do. You both need time before you make any permanent decision about where she will live. If she is in hospital, it may be that after a short stay she will be able to return home and manage with some extra support from social services. Maybe her home can be altered or adapted so that she can carry on living there. Or she may be able to live independently in a sheltered flat or bungalow.

Even if it becomes clear that she can no longer manage on her own, it is best to give yourselves time to consider the options. Chapter 2 looks at some of the alternatives to care in a residential or nursing home.

Emergency care arrangements

If your relative has had an accident or been taken suddenly ill and neither you nor another member of your family can look after her, then you may need to make emergency care arrangements to make sure that she is safe and properly looked after for the next few days.

3

To help you make emergency arrangements, you should contact:

- your relative's GP – she or he will arrange for admission to hospital if necessary;
- the social services department for the area where your relative lives.

Social services departments

The social services department (called the social work department in Scotland) is part of your local authority or council (look in the telephone directory under the name of the local authority). Your local authority could be:

- a county (such as Devon or Lincolnshire);
- a metropolitan borough (or district) such as Tameside or Rotherham;
- a London borough (such as Haringey or Sutton).

All social services departments are organised differently, and the jobs people do have different names in different parts of the country. Most social services departments have a head office and a number of areas or districts. Within each district there may be several smaller teams covering local communities. It will usually be the local team which arranges care services for your relative.

Social services should make an assessment of your relative's needs, as explained on pages 12–16. Stress that it is an emergency, and if there is nobody with your relative looking after her, make sure they are aware of the fact.

They may be able to arrange temporary care for your relative, either in her own home or in a residential or nursing home. (Most care homes are happy to accept people on a temporary basis, provided they have room. But you need to be clear about how much notice they want before your relative leaves. Otherwise you may find you have to pay the fees even after your relative has left.)

The local authority may also be able to help towards the cost if your relative's income and savings are below a certain amount. (The value of your relative's home will not be taken into consideration if her stay in a care home is only temporary – say, less than a year (see pp 61–62). You must make it clear to social services that this is a temporary arrangement.)

If social services cannot help, you could try:

■ getting a friend, neighbour or relation who lives close by to drop in regularly to keep an eye on your relative;

■ getting help through a voluntary scheme such as Crossroads Care (address on p 85) or a private care agency (contact the United Kingdom Home Care Association – address on p 88);

■ inviting her to live with you or another family member for a while;

■ you or another family member going to stay with her.

Whatever plans you make at this stage, it is important that everyone involved is quite clear that it is only a temporary arrangement. If possible, set aside a definite time for working out a long-term solution.

For more *i*nformation

i *The Carer's Handbook: What to do and who to turn to*, published by Age Concern Books (details on p 90).

If your relative is being discharged from hospital

If someone has been in hospital and is being discharged, the family may find themselves under great pressure either to take her home to live with them or to find a suitable care home.

There should be a properly set out hospital discharge procedure. Government guidance is set out in *NHS responsibilities for meeting continuing health care needs* (HSG(95)8). The Department of Health's *Hospital Discharge Workbook* published in 1994 is referred to in this guidance. Health and local authorities must have in place arrangements to provide services for people being discharged from hospital, to enable them to either return home with support or to move to other appropriate care. This should involve a multi-disciplinary assessment of the patient's needs before discharge, identifying which services are to be provided by the NHS and which by social services. For those returning home with support, part of the assessment may involve a home visit with an occupational therapist. Any decisions about the services needed should be given to the patient in writing (or other appropriate recorded form), together with a copy of the needs assessment.

Problems can occur for older people and their relatives if they are put under undue pressure to make their own arrangements to place their relative in a home. But the health authority may have responsibilities to provide continuing care for her free of charge under the NHS. Such care may be provided in a long-stay hospital ward or in a nursing home run by the health authority or, increasingly, in a bed in a private or voluntary nursing home purchased by the health authority.

Government guidelines (HSG(95)8) also set out a wide range of continuing health care services which the NHS should provide. This includes NHS continuing inpatient care – that is, care which the NHS funds in full. Each health authority must set and publish its own criteria for these services.

Before the patient is discharged, a decision should be taken as to whether she meets her health authority's criteria for NHS continuing inpatient care. If she does not, then she may have to move to a residential or nursing home and pay towards the costs. However, the patient and her family cannot be forced to find a place or contribute towards the cost except in exceptional circumstances. But no-one has the right to insist on staying in hospital indefinitely.

Roshan

'Mother made amazing progress while she was in the stroke unit. When she went in she couldn't even stand up, but in a few weeks they got her walking with the help of a Zimmer frame. Then the consultant said they had done all they could, and started pressuring us to move her. I suppose he needed the bed. I knew she couldn't come to live with me, because I can't lift her on my own – I'm too small – and she often falls. We desperately started to look for a home, but there were no vacancies in the ones we liked. The social worker pleaded with the consultant, and so did the nurse and physiotherapist, but he wouldn't listen. He had her transferred to a geriatric ward. She was confused before, but that made her even worse. She kept saying, "Please could anyone tell me where I live now." It was pitiful. In the end, we found a place in a home we were happy with, but it was a long way to travel. It was far from ideal, but really we were under so much pressure we felt we had no choice.'

People may feel they want to challenge the health authority's decision if they believe they, or their relative, should be getting the sort of care which only the NHS can provide.

If you believe that your relative does meet the health authority's criteria for NHS continuing inpatient care, then you – or your relative – have the right to ask the health authority to review this decision before your relative is discharged from hospital. Information about this review procedure should be available from the hospital. If you are seeking a review, you may want to contact your local Community Health Council (Health Council in Scotland) or Age Concern England for further advice.

At the same time, do not feel pressured into agreeing to care for your relative yourself or to take on financial responsibilities to pay for her care if you do not want to do so.

For more *i*nformation

ⓘ Age Concern England Factsheet 37 *Hospital discharge arrangements and NHS continuing health care services.*

*D*eciding whether a care home is necessary

Having made temporary arrangements, you and you relative now have time to take stock of the situation. The **flowchart** on page 9 will give you some idea of the possibilities. (Some of the alternatives to residential or nursing home care are discussed in the next chapter.) There are four main factors you need to look at:

7

- your relative's preference, and the feelings of other people involved;
- your relative's health, both physical and mental;
- how much she is at risk, or how much risk she presents to others, if she carries on living at home;
- the alternatives available to her.

Your relative's preference

The following are just some of the advantages and drawbacks of care homes that you and your relative might want to consider. There may be others which apply to your particular circumstances.

Possible advantages

- Safety: someone is always there.
- Round-the-clock care.
- Good facilities.
- No worries about upkeep of the house, bills, etc.
- Possible companionship.
- Peace of mind for both of you – less worry for you and less feeling that she is a burden for your relative. This could mean a chance to enjoy your relationship without stress.

Possible drawbacks

- Unfamiliar surroundings.
- Loss of independence and some loss of privacy.
- Inadequate care and lack of stimulation.
- Loneliness and loss of contact with family, friends, neighbours.
- Your relative may feel unwanted and unloved.
- Family may feel guilty.
- Expense: if your relative has savings over £16,000 she may have to pay the full cost (see pp 55–56).
- Difficulty of finding a place in a home that will accept someone with your relative's disability.
- Difficulty of finding a home your relative likes.

Flowchart

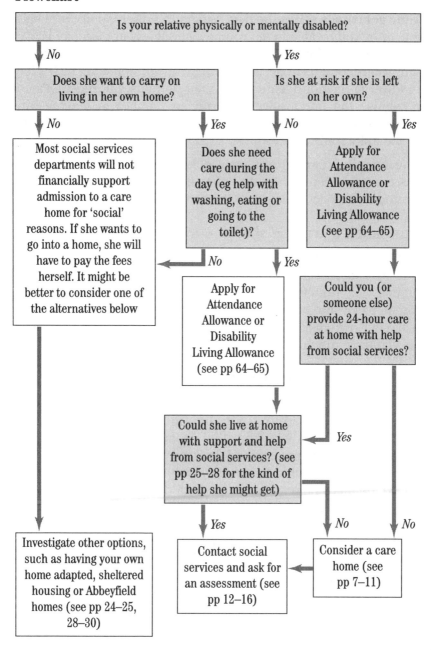

Your relative's health

Your relative's GP is the best person to talk to about her health. She or he will be able to tell you how her illness or disability is likely to progress, and what the long-term prospects are. This is important where long-term decisions are involved. Remember, GPs have to observe the confidentiality of their patients, but most GPs now recognise the importance of involving families in making long-term decisions, especially when the person involved is physically or mentally frail.

The hospital consultant who looked after your relative, if she has recently been in hospital, may also be able to give you information and advice, subject to the same rules of confidentiality.

How much at risk is she?

Sometimes an older person who is mentally sound but physically frail may know that she will be at risk if she lives independently, but she may prefer to take the risk. It is up to her – she cannot be forced to go into a care home. If someone is too mentally frail to make her own decisions, however, then the family and professionals will have to make the decision for her.

What are the alternatives?

In the past, an older person and her family could decide for themselves that she would like to go into a care home, and she could often get financial help from the Department of Social Security, depending on her income and savings. However, since the 1990 NHS and Community Care Act (which came into force in April 1993), financial help with the cost from the local authority will only be available if their social services department thinks the person _needs_ to be in a care home. So you may find that your relative does not have the choice of going into a care home, unless the social services department accepts that there is no better alternative. This is why it is important to contact social services and ask for an assessment of your relative's needs. There is more about this in the section on the social services assessment on pages 12–16.

People who can afford to pay the full fees of a care home themselves will not have their choices affected in this way. But problems can arise if your relative's funds run out while she is in the home, as explained on page 55.

Nowadays, the emphasis in most social services departments is very much on keeping people living independently for as long as possible and providing care in their own home, rather than admitting them to a care home. Generally the person from social services who assesses your relative's needs will recommend a care home only if they think that it would be impossible to provide sufficient services to enable her to carry on living on her own. The person doing the assessment may also recommend a care home if your relative is living with someone else, and that person can no longer cope or is under too much stress.

It is much more likely that social services will be able to arrange for a person with physical disabilities to be cared for at home than a person who is severely mentally ill. Someone who suffers from dementia may need day and night supervision, which could be difficult to arrange except in a care home.

Every local authority has its own criteria for admitting an older person to a care home. This is something you could discuss with the person who is carrying out the assessment.

A social worker is often a good person to advise you and your relative about the available alternatives. Sometimes a social worker will help you to reach your own decisions, without trying to impose one particular solution on you; but sometimes social workers have very strong views about what should happen, which may be different to yours or your relative's. In this case, you might find it helpful to get support from another professional, such as a doctor or district nurse, or from a voluntary organisation such as Age Concern or the Alzheimer's Disease Society (addresses on pp 89 and 83) or a Citizens Advice Bureau.

The social services assessment

Under the 1990 NHS and Community Care Act, the local authority social services department has a duty to assess the needs of *anyone* who seems to be in need of community care services which they might arrange or provide, and to make a decision about what services, if any, they will arrange for them.

The social services assessment is the key to all community care social services – both residential and nursing home care and care for people living in their own homes. Once your relative's needs have been assessed, it is up to social services to arrange any social services that they decide are necessary. If, during the assessment, social services find that your relative also has health or housing needs, she should be referred to the appropriate authority.

The assessment is to help find out:

- what your relative feels she needs and, where appropriate, what you (as her carer) feel;
- whether she can manage to live in her own home (or in the carer's home) if enough help is provided;
- how much help she needs and what sort of help is most suitable;
- whether she needs to be in a residential or nursing home;
- how much she should pay towards the cost of care at home or in a residential or nursing home.

If your relative has sufficient funds to pay for residential or nursing home care herself, then there is no need to involve social services, though you may still find a social worker's expertise and knowledge very helpful. In particular, they may be able to help you contact the NHS, to see if any health services will be available to you in the home.

If she does need help with the fees, or you think she may need help with the fees in future, then it is essential to involve social services at an early stage. If your relative's funds run out while she is in the home, you cannot assume that the social services department will automatically pick up the bill. They will want to assess your relative, and they will use the same criteria as if she were going into a care home for the first time. So it is still a good idea to ask for an assessment, even if you know your relative will be paying the cost herself. There is more about this on pages 55–56.

Arranging an assessment

Anyone can ask social services to carry out an assessment. Your relative's GP, the district nurse, or a friend or neighbour may already have alerted the local social services department to your relative's situation. But if they haven't, then you or your relative can simply ring up the local social services department, ask to speak to the duty officer, and explain that you would like your relative to be assessed and why. Social services may want to make sure that, whenever appropriate, you have your relative's permission to contact them. If your relative is in hospital, you should contact the hospital social worker.

Social services departments are not obliged to assess everyone who requests this. By law, they must assess people with a substantial and permanent disability, and they must also assess anyone who appears to need the sorts of services they arrange or provide.

Someone from the social services department – it might be a social worker or an assistant or a specially trained assessor – should visit your relative at home (if she is in hospital they may talk to her on the ward, probably near the time she is due to be discharged). They will ask questions about her personal circumstances and her health problems, and about what tasks she finds difficult. They will decide what care they are able or willing to arrange by comparing her assessed needs with the eligibility criteria they have set for different services. Once a decision has been made, they may also ask about her financial situation to see how much, if anything, she should pay towards the cost of these services.

They may also ask the hospital doctor or her GP about her health, and how her illness or disability is likely to develop in the future.

Your relative may want to have someone with her during the assessment, especially if she is mentally frail.

If your relative is living with someone else who looks after her – a spouse or another family member – then they can be involved in the assessment too. Under the Carers (Recognition and Services) Act 1995, which became law from April 1996, carers also have the right to ask for their *own* assessment, to see what help and support might be available for them, if they provide – or intend to provide – substantial and regular care. Their assessment takes place when the person they care for is being assessed or reassessed.

If your relative's health or situation changes after her assessment, she can ring up and ask to be reassessed, or you can ring up on her behalf.

What questions will they ask?

Many people are understandably worried at the idea of being questioned by a stranger about their personal lives. In fact the person who does the assessment, whether it is a social worker or a special assessor or someone else, should have been trained to put people at their ease.

The questions your relative is asked may depend on how much care the assessor thinks will be needed. If it seems as though your relative will need a lot of care, then the questions should be more detailed. Some social services departments carry out a preliminary assessment, consisting of a few straightforward questions, to establish whether a full and detailed assessment is needed.

According to Department of Health guidance, a full assessment should usually include questions about:

Biographical details Age, family circumstances, ethnic origin, religion, etc.

What help your relative thinks she needs.

How well she can manage Can she look after herself, and cope with everyday tasks such as getting washed and dressed, eating, walking around, going up and down stairs?

Her health, both physical and mental They may consult the doctor at the hospital or your relative's GP, health visitor or district nurse for more information.

Medicines Does your relative need to take medicines regularly, and does this cause any problems?

Lifestyle, abilities, culture, ethnic background, and personal factors such as bereavement: how do these affect your relative's view of her situation and her ability to cope?

Whether there is a carer A carer should be consulted as well, and if necessary have his or her own needs assessed.

Who else is around to help Friends, neighbours, other family members, etc.

What help she is getting already From social services or other agencies.

Her housing situation Does your relative want to stay where she is? If so, does her house need to be adapted in any way? Or is she thinking of moving into sheltered housing or a care home?

Transport Does she have difficulty in getting to the shops, doctor, etc?

Whether she is at risk Does she suffer from an illness which might cause her to collapse suddenly, for example diabetes, epilepsy, heart failure? Has she had a number of falls or other accidents or 'near misses' at home? Does she perhaps put others at risk by strange, threatening or erratic behaviour? (Sometimes people with Alzheimer's disease turn on the gas and then forget to light it – a risk both to themselves and to neighbours.)

Finance What income and savings does your relative have, and what benefits is she claiming? They may ask for proof, such as her pension book, or bank or building society statements. They will probably try to make sure that your relative is claiming all the benefits she is entitled to. In general, though, you do not need to give financial details initially. The care assessment and the financial assessment should be done separately (see pp 55–62 on financial assessments).

In practice, however, assessments are not always as detailed or as thorough as this because it would take so long to carry them out. It may therefore be worth you and your relative thinking in advance about what points you want to cover. If, for example, your relative wants to stay at home but transport to the doctor and shopping is a problem, make sure you make that point.

Above all, if you feel that you haven't had a fair hearing, or if your point of view seems to be being ignored, you should say so and persist.

If you are not happy with the assessment

Unfortunately, in practice local authorities are sometimes not able to offer people all the care they need. They may not even assess someone as having needs which they know they cannot meet.

If you or your relative is not happy with the result of the assessment or the way it was carried out, don't be afraid to complain. Local authorities are required by law to have a complaints procedure. All you have to do is ring up the social services department, explain that you would like to make a complaint, and ask them to put you through to the right person. However, before you do that, it is usually better to raise the matter first with the person involved, or with the team leader for the area in which your relative lives. Either way, social services should be able to give you a leaflet explaining the complaints procedure.

Remember, you are more likely to be successful if you remain polite – however upset or angry you may feel. It is also a good idea to think very carefully about what you want to say before you pick up the phone. You may be able to get advice and support from a voluntary organisation – such as Age Concern or the Alzheimer's Disease Society (addresses on pp 89 and 83), or the Citizens Advice Bureau, to help you make your complaint.

For more *i*nformation

i Age Concern England Factsheet 41 *Local authority assessments for community care services.*

Talking it over

There is no getting away from the fact that many – probably most – older people initially say they do not want to go into a care home. Yet over a period of time, there often comes a realisation that it may be the best or even the only option.

Robert

'Mother didn't particularly want to go into a home. But we didn't really have a choice. There was nothing else any of us could do.'

Those who reach this position of their own accord, without being pressured by their family or doctor, are more likely to take a positive approach to their new life in the home, and to settle happily.

Going into a care home is such an emotive issue that just talking about it can upset people, and all kinds of misunderstandings can arise. People may feel torn between conflicting emotions such as love and guilt, other commitments, deep-rooted resentments, even financial considerations. Problems can arise when:

■ Family members or professional workers feel that your relative will be at risk unless she goes into a care home, but your relative feels that she would rather take the risk than give up her independence.

■ Your relative does not want to upset her family or the person carrying out the assessment, so goes along with suggestions she is not really happy with. Her resentment may come out in other ways, which may seem to you to be niggling about trivial things.

■ Professionals, such as doctors or social workers, put pressure on her or on the family to accept solutions which don't feel right. Other members of the family may put pressure on too.

■ Your relative is too confused or mentally frail to take part in decision-making at all. This often makes it harder for the rest of the family, as they have to guess at her feelings as well as wrestling with their own.

There is no easy way to resolve all these conflicts. The important thing is that everyone has the chance to say what is really on their mind, and everyone gets a fair hearing.

Feelings about care homes

Often our feelings about care homes reach right back into childhood, to our relationship with our parents. If the relationship was close, we may feel upset to see them suffering. We may find it painful to see them frail or mentally disturbed, or feel upset that we cannot give them the care they gave us. If our relationship with our parents was difficult, we may still feel anger and resentment against them, and we may not want to look after them; we may also feel guilty about reacting in this way. Most people feel a complex mixture of all these. And even when we know there is really no choice, it still doesn't stop us feeling guilty and upset.

Joe

'My mother was born and grew up in the Caribbean. I could never let her go into a home – she would have no one to share her memories with.'

Shirley

'I love my mother dearly, but she drives me crazy. I couldn't live with her.'

For the older person, too, thinking about a care home can raise some deep anxieties. Beneath concerns about accommodation, food and facilities may lurk deeper worries:

- Will they treat me kindly?
- Will they respect me for who I am?
- Will they understand and put up with my little habits and foibles?
- Will my partner be able to manage without me?
- What will happen to my house/garden/pets? Will I ever see them again?

The main thing is to recognise these feelings and not try to sweep them under the carpet. Your and your relative's feelings are important – just as important as the practical questions. After all, it's no good agreeing that the best solution is for your grandfather to move in with you if you know in your heart of hearts that it's going to drive you mad. And it's no good allowing the doctor to persuade your mother to go into a care home if you both know you would be happier living together.

It isn't easy to get the right balance between emotional and practical considerations. But being clear about what everybody feels, and what the practical possibilities are, can make it easier.

Other people to talk to

Involving other people is important at this stage, both friends and relations and professionals such as the GP and social worker.

A counsellor may be able to help you to get your own feelings in perspective, without trying to impose their own solution. You could get referred to a counsellor through your GP or through MIND or the British Association for Counselling (addresses on pp 87 and 84).

Voluntary organisations and specialist charities can be a good source of impartial advice and information. Some charities offer specialised information about particular illnesses or disabilities. Others, such as Age Concern, are concerned with the welfare of older people generally, and may be able to advise you about help and services available in your area. There is a list of useful addresses on pages 83–88.

For more *i*nformation

🛈 *Getting on with Homes* by Dorothy White, available from the Relatives Association (address on p 87).

🛈 *Relative Views: 65 relatives comment on the good and sometimes not so good aspects of homes for older people*, available from the Relatives Association (address on p 87).

ⓘ From Home to Home: A study of older people's hopes, expectations and experiences of residential care, available from Counsel and Care (address on p 85).

ⓘ The Carer's Handbook: What to do and who to turn to, published by Age Concern Books (details on p 90).

2 What are the alternatives to a care home?

Many older people would prefer not to go into a care home, but think that there is no alternative. In fact there is a great range of services and accommodation available which could help them carry on living independently.

The 1990 NHS and Community Care Act gave local authorities the responsibility of assessing people who seem to need care, and deciding what kind of care would be best for them. The Act encourages local authorities to provide services that allow people to carry on living independently, and to suggest a care home only when there is no suitable alternative. This means that there should now be better support in the community for someone staying in her own home, or living with a relative, or moving into sheltered housing.

This chapter looks at some of the alternatives to residential or nursing home care for you and your relative to consider before you make your decision.

Sophie

'It made all the difference. It meant that Mum could spend the last years of her life at home, rather than in a care home.'

'Mum was admitted to a residential home when she was discharged from hospital, but she wanted to come home. So Dad and I contacted social services to see what help they could offer. We'd heard about home helps and meals on wheels, but we didn't realise how much things had changed. They didn't have home helps any more, they'd subcontracted the service to a local charity. And the meals on wheels was subcontracted to a private firm that delivered them once a week, prepacked for the freezer. But although they didn't provide the service any more, they helped to arrange it all for Mum and Dad, and she only had to pay a fixed amount based on her income.

'They also arranged for a wonderful woman to come round in the morning to help her get up and get washed and dressed, and someone else to come in the evening to help her get to bed.

'It made all the difference. It meant that Mum could spend the last years of her life at home, rather than in a care home.'

Staying in her own home or living with you

Your relative might be able to carry on living independently with the right help and support. People such as home care assistants or home care workers (home helps) and services such as day centres or meals on wheels could make all the difference to an elderly person living in her own home, and to her family trying to care for her.

If your relative would like to stay at home but needs help in order to manage, the local social services department (called the social work department in Scotland) should carry out an assessment of her needs, as explained on pages 12–16. The checklist on pages 25–28 gives you an idea of the sorts of social services and health care services that might be offered to help your relative.

If the social services department does decide to help her, the services offered will be arranged by them but they may not all be provided by them. Some are provided by voluntary organisations and some are run privately.

If the person carrying out the assessment finds that there is a health problem that your relative's GP does not know about, they should inform the GP, with your relative's permission. Where appropriate, both health and housing authorities may be invited to participate in the assessment.

If you or your relative can afford to pay for help for your relative yourselves, you do not have to involve the social services department. But it may still be worth doing, because the person doing the assessment should know what is available in the area.

If your relative comes to live in your home, or in an annexe at your home (a 'granny' flat), or you go to live in hers, she may still be able to get some support services, but it is as well to check with the local authority before you commit yourselves.

Rose

'Last time I went to visit them, I was suddenly struck by how very frail they were. We talked about going to live near them. We have both retired, and our children have grown up and left home, so there is nothing in particular to keep us in this town. When they heard we were thinking of coming to live nearby they were so excited.'

For more *i*nformation

i Age Concern England Factsheet 6 *Finding help at home.*

i Counsel and Care Factsheet 18 *Community care services for older people.*

i *The Community Care Handbook: The reformed system explained*, published by Age Concern Books (details on p 91).

i *The Carer's Handbook: What to do and who to turn to*, published by Age Concern Books (details on p 90).

i *Caring at Home: A handbook for people looking after someone at home* by Nancy Kohner, published by the National Extension College and the King's Fund (Tel: 01223 316644).

i *Who Cares Now? Caring for an older person* by Nancy Kohner and Penny Mares, published by BBC Education.

Altering or adapting your home

It is worth taking a good look at your relative's home (or your home if she is coming to live with you) and seeing if there are any changes which could make it safer or more convenient to live in.

General repairs and improvements such as damp-proofing and insulation may be needed, or maybe the house could be adapted to the needs of a disabled person by adding, for example:

- ramps leading up to doors with steps;
- a stronger stair rail;
- grab-rails by doors, and in the bathroom and toilet;
- wider doorways to allow for a wheelchair;
- extra heating, or more convenient heating;
- a downstairs toilet and/or bathroom;
- a walk-in shower;
- a stair lift or other internal lift.

Getting advice

If your relative has a disability, the best person to advise about any alterations to her home is an **occupational therapist (OT)**. OTs are trained to look at how people with disabilities manage everyday tasks, such as getting about, washing, using the toilet, cooking, preparing drinks and eating, and to suggest ways these could be made easier. OTs can be based either in a hospital or in the social services department of your local council. However, in some areas you may have to wait for a long time for a visit from an OT.

Agencies called **Care and Repair** or **Staying Put** have been set up in some areas to advise older people and people with disabilities about repairing and adapting their homes. To find out whether there is a scheme near where your relative lives, look in the telephone directory, ask the local housing department, or contact Care and Repair (address on p 84).

Grants from the council

Your relative may be able to get a grant from the local council towards the cost of improvements and alterations. If she has a disability, she may be eligible for a **disabled facilities grant**. This will depend on her income and savings.

The council's **private housing grants section** can advise you or your relative about grants and work out whether she qualifies. If your relative is a tenant, they can advise her landlord about applying.

For more *i*nformation

i Age Concern England Factsheet 13 *Older home owners: financial help with repairs and adaptations.*

i *A Buyer's Guide to Retirement Housing*, published by Age Concern Books (details on p 92).

i Age Concern England Factsheet 33 *Feeling safer at home and outside.*

Checklist of support services at home

Help with the daily routine	Whom to contact
Help with housework, shopping, cleaning	*Social services, voluntary organisation or private agency*
Help with getting up, getting washed and dressed, going to the toilet, eating, getting undressed, going to bed	*Social services or voluntary care attendant scheme (eg Crossroads Care) or private agency (contact United Kingdom Home Care Association)*
Help with incontinence or incontinence supplies (pads, pants, bedding)	*District nurse or continence adviser (ask the GP)*
Help with bathing, toileting, lifting	*Social services, district nurse (ask the GP) or private agency*
Laundry service	*Social services (many areas no longer offer this service) or private laundry service (look in the Yellow Pages)*

Help with meals	**Whom to contact**
Meals on wheels	*Social services or voluntary organisation (eg Age Concern or WRVS – Women's Royal Voluntary Service)*
Luncheon club	*Social services, local community group, church or voluntary group*

Help with medical problems	**Whom to contact**
Advice about most general health problems	*Your relative's GP; who may refer her to someone else*
Nursing care at home, eg injections, changing dressings, etc	*District nurse (ask the GP) or private nursing agency*
Advice about lifting or turning someone heavy	*District nurse or physiotherapist (ask the GP)*
Advice on mobility and exercise	*Physiotherapist (ask the GP)*

Help with aids, equipment and home adaptations	**Whom to contact**
Advice on equipment to help with everyday living, eg washing, cooking, using the toilet	*Occupational therapist (social services or hospital), disability living centre (contact the Disability Living Centres Council or the Disabled Living Foundation). Some shops also sell equipment*
Advice on aids to help with sensory impairment (sight, hearing, speech)	*Social services, speech therapist, RNIB or RNID, or Disabled Living Foundation*
Equipment for bedroom, bathroom (rails, hoist, etc)	*District nurse or occupational therapist (social services)*
Mobility aids, eg wheelchair, walking sticks, walking frames	*GP, physiotherapist or hospital (ask the GP)*

| Short-term hire of equipment | *British Red Cross (ask at your local branch), local Age Concern group, WRVS or other voluntary organisation* |
| Advice on home security measures | *Police or Age Concern* |

Help with getting about	**Whom to contact**
Help with transport	*Dial-a-ride or other voluntary organisation, social services or private taxi*
Transport to and from voluntary luncheon club, day centre, hospital, doctor, etc	*Social services or community group*
Transport to shops	*Community or voluntary group, Good Neighbour scheme (ask at social services). Some large stores run a free bus service*
Advice about getting a specially adapted car	*Motability, Department of Social Security*
Orange parking badge	*Social services*
Disabled Person's Railcard	*Local railway station*

Social activities	**Whom to contact**
Day centre, luncheon club or social club	*Social services, voluntary organisation (eg local Age Concern or Alzheimer's Disease Society group) or community centre*
Holidays	*Social services or voluntary group (eg Carers National Association), Holiday Care Service*
Leisure facilities, such as mobile library (including large print books and books on tape), talking newspapers, adult education classes	*Local library, local education department, Talking Newspapers Association, Calibre*

27

A break for the carer (respite care)	Whom to contact
Someone to sit with your relative while you go out for a few hours, or to stay overnight or for a weekend	*Social services or voluntary organisation (eg Crossroads Care) or private agency (contact United Kingdom Home Care Association)*
Day care for your relative in a special day centre; may include lunch, social activities, use of bathing facilities, chiropody, hairdressing, etc	*Social services, hospital or voluntary organisation (eg Age Concern, Help the Aged or Alzheimer's Disease Society)*
Short-term residential care, from a day to a fortnight. Could be in a hospital or residential home, or even with another family	*Social services, hospital, private or voluntary residential or nursing home*

Sheltered housing

Sheltered housing may be ideal for older people or people with disabilities who are fairly independent but want the security of having someone there to keep an eye on them.

There are many different kinds of sheltered housing scheme, providing different levels of care. In some schemes, a warden is there all the time, who may also arrange for shopping, home help/home care and other services. In other schemes, the warden just drops in daily or once in a while to check that residents are all right, and other arrangements have to be made individually by the residents. In some areas there are purpose built developments of flats or bungalows which are specially designed to suit older people or people with disabilities, but with no warden.

A big advantage of sheltered housing is that the units are quite small and easy to heat and look after, so your relative will not have to worry about heating or maintenance bills. Accommodation is usually all on one level, though not always on the ground floor. If it is important for your relative to be on the ground floor, you should check that a bungalow or ground floor flat is available.

Most sheltered housing is in purpose-built developments of bungalows and flats, rented from the local council or a housing association.

There are sheltered housing schemes which cater specially for people of a particular religious or ethnic group, though these may not be in the area where you or your relative lives. To find out about them, you could make enquiries through your community leaders or your religious or ethnic network, or contact one of the organisations listed on pages 43–44.

Sheltered housing to rent

The best way to find out about sheltered housing to rent is to contact the local council to ask if they could consider an application. If not, they may be able to send you a list of housing associations which have sheltered housing in the area. Lists by county of housing associations with accommodation for older people are also available from Age Concern England (address on p 89).

Many housing associations allocate 50 per cent or even 100 per cent of their properties to people nominated by the local council. To nominate someone, the council must be satisfied that they are a 'high priority' for sheltered housing.

Sheltered housing to buy

In some areas, there are private sheltered housing schemes where you can buy a unit, either from a housing association or from a private company. It is very important, if you are thinking of buying into one of these schemes, to find out exactly what is included in the purchase price and what extras there are. You could find that the weekly outgoings are almost as much as paying rent.

Abbeyfield houses

Abbeyfield houses are another popular alternative. These are large houses with bedsits for up to about ten older people and a resident housekeeper. Meals are provided, which means the cost may be a little higher than in ordinary sheltered housing. For some people, Abbeyfield houses offer the best of both worlds, combining privacy and independence with social and practical support. They are usually more suitable for fairly active and independent people, but some Abbeyfield houses now provide care for more dependent people. The Abbeyfield Society is a registered charity. For more information contact the address on page 83.

For more *i*nformation

❶ Age Concern England Factsheet 2 *Retirement housing for sale.*

❶ Age Concern England Factsheet 8 *Moving into rented housing.*

❶ *A Buyer's Guide to Retirement Housing*, published by Age Concern Books (details on p 92).

3 Which kind of care home?

Choosing a care home can be quite bewildering. There are so many different homes, with different facilities, levels of care, fees, decor and furnishings and much more. Each has its own atmosphere and philosophy and rules and regulations. Each home provides a different experience and quality of life for its residents.

The kind of care home that suits your relative will depend first and foremost on the level of care she needs. This chapter looks at the three main categories of care home: residential homes, nursing homes and dual-registered homes.

It explains what the homes are and are not likely to provide, and how they are registered. Once you and your relative have decided what kind of home is right for her needs, see Chapter 4 on how to choose between the homes that are available.

Robert

'We felt under great pressure to find somewhere that would accept her before her condition deteriorated too much'

Robert's mother was becoming increasingly confused, but the family couldn't agree whether she needed to be in a care home, or what sort of home she should be in. Robert felt that his mother needed a residential home where she would be safe and staff could keep an eye on her rather

31

than actual nursing care. But he found that many residential homes were reluctant to take someone with dementia, because they need such a lot of looking after. They looked at one excellent home, but it was full. The next home said she was too confused to fit in with the other residents.

'They said we might need to look for a nursing home. We felt under great pressure to find somewhere that would accept her before her condition deteriorated too much. So when the next home said they would take her, we just accepted. But when we took her round to move in, our hearts sank. It was like something out of a nightmare – the residents all sitting round the edge of the room, strapped into their chairs, staring into space and drooling.

'Well, we steeled ourselves and left her there. She was so confused she didn't know what was happening. We felt awful. That night we couldn't sleep a wink. My sister and I phoned each other up and talked all night. In the morning, we drove round to the home, picked her up, and brought her back with us.

'We started to search all over again. We got addresses from social services; from people we knew, and even from the *Yellow Pages*. Then we rang every single one up, and took down details of those which had vacancies and would accept someone with dementia. We ended up with a shortlist of about six and set out to visit them all.

'We knew immediately that this home was the right one. There was a good mix of people – some were very dependent, but some had simply retired. And we took an instant liking to the matron. Although it wasn't registered as a nursing home, she obviously understood mother's condition and knew she would get worse. She said that once they accepted a resident they made a commitment to look after them as long as they could – not to pass them on to a nursing home when things became difficult but to look after them to the end of their life if possible.'

What level of care does your relative need?

What kind of care home is best for your relative will depend on how much care she needs. Before you and she can choose a care home, you need to be clear whether she just needs help with personal care (washing, dressing, eating, going to the toilet, etc) or whether she needs nursing from a qualified nurse.

When your relative's care needs are assessed (see pp 12–16), the person doing the assessment should make clear what kind of care they believe your relative needs.

Nursing homes are generally more expensive than residential homes, so the social services department will not pay the full cost of nursing home care if they think your relative only needs to be in a residential home. If you are not sure what level of care your relative has been assessed as needing, you can ring social services and ask. If you and your relative have decided not to have her assessed by social services because she is paying for the full cost of the care home herself, your relative's GP is the best person to advise whether nursing care is needed, or is likely to be needed in the near future.

There are basically three kinds of care home to choose from.

Residential homes

What they provide

Residential homes – sometimes also referred to as **rest homes** or **retirement homes** – provide the sort of routine daily care that you or another family member could provide: help with getting up in the morning and going to bed at night; help with getting dressed, going to the toilet and having a bath; help with meals. Some residential homes will accept people who are incontinent of urine, but this is something you should check.

33

There should be specially adapted facilities such as baths, showers and toilets. The accommodation should be easily accessible to wheelchairs.

If it is not all on the same level, there should be ramps and lifts. There will be communal areas for dining and sitting, and there may be a communal garden or outdoor area where residents can sit in the summer.

The home may also provide companionship, a feeling of security, social activities, and personal services such as hairdressing and chiropody (though these may be charged as 'extras' if they are not NHS treatments). For a confused or demented person, it may provide supervision in a safe environment. But if your relative is very confused, the home may decide that it cannot meet her needs and will recommend that you look for a nursing home.

What they don't provide

A residential home is not suitable for someone who needs skilled nursing care from a qualified nurse. Sometimes it is not easy to define the difference between nursing care and personal care. It will be up to the discretion of the person in charge of the home to say if they don't think they can cope with your relative's needs. Unfortunately some homes may be reluctant to take people who they think will need a lot of care because they think it will put more pressure on their staff, even if they do not need skilled nursing care.

If your relative is a borderline case, you may well find that while one residential home will not accept her, another will be happy to have her. However, it is important to be honest about what your relative's care needs are, and to ask the home how long they think they will be able to continue looking after her. Otherwise you may find that she soon has to move to a different home which can provide more care, and this may be upsetting and disruptive for her.

Who runs them

In many areas, most residential homes are run privately or by voluntary sector organisations – charities, religious and ethnic groups, friendly societies and trusts. Some voluntary homes give priority to people who belong to a particular ethnic, religious or social group, regardless of where they live. Local authorities also run their own homes, but they can arrange for someone to be cared for in any type of home, as long as it is suitable for their needs.

How they are registered

Residential homes that cater for four or more elderly people have to be registered with the local authority under the Registered Homes Act 1984, and have to be inspected twice a year. The Act lays down strict rules about accommodation, staffing levels and care provided. The registration certificate, which must be prominently displayed in the home, will say how many and what type of residents the home can accept.

Local authorities have to make public their inspection reports on homes they visit. You can ask your social worker or the Inspection Unit at your local social services department where you can see the reports.

In England and Wales, smaller homes, catering for three people or fewer, have a simplified registration and inspection procedure under the Registered Homes (Amendment) Act 1991. If you and your relative decide that she would prefer a smaller home, it is important that you satisfy yourselves about the quality of care, and that you keep a regular check on your relative's well-being.

Nursing homes

What they provide

Nursing homes are for people who need skilled nursing care. As well as the facilities found in residential homes, they offer round-the-clock nursing, and they have to be run by a qualified nurse or doctor. For this reason they tend to be more expensive than residential homes.

Residents in nursing homes are more likely to be bedridden, or unable to get about without a great deal of help. Or they may have medical conditions which require frequent attention from a nurse or a doctor.

Katy

'My sister and I went to look at a couple of residential homes. We didn't like the first one, and the second one was not suitable for someone in a wheelchair. Then we heard about a new nursing home opening. The doctor told us that before the end of the year she would be so disabled that she would need 24-hour nursing care. So we decided to go for that one.'

What they don't provide

Nursing homes should have enough qualified staff to be able to provide round-the-clock nursing care to all their residents. However, some homes, especially those operating with the legal minimum of qualified staff, may be reluctant to accept residents who will require a great deal of care. For example, families of people with very severe dementia sometimes report that they have difficulty in finding a nursing home that will accept their relative.

Margaret

'Really, we had no choice at all. Mother was so severely demented that none of the residential homes would take her, and there was only one nursing home that had a vacancy.'

Who runs them

By law, a nursing home has to be managed by a qualified nurse or doctor. But of course the actual owner of the home does not have to be medically qualified. Most nursing homes are run privately as businesses by individuals or companies. There are also many nursing homes run on a non-profit-making basis by voluntary organisations. Some of these cater for people of a particular religious or ethnic group, some for members of particular trades or professions, some for people with a particular illness or disability.

Very occasionally health authorities run their own nursing homes as an alternative to long-stay hospital wards, or they 'buy' beds in a nursing home which they make available to long-term patients.

How they are registered

All nursing homes that provide nursing care for more than one patient must by law be registered with the Health Authority (Health Board in Scotland) and inspected at least twice a year. The registration certificate, stating the maximum number of people the home can care for, must be displayed in a conspicuous place. It is planned that Health Authorities will have to make public their inspection reports on the homes they visit.

Dual-registered homes

Dual-registered homes combine the services of residential and nursing homes under one roof. They provide the ordinary personal care offered by residential homes, and they also have some beds where they can provide round-the-clock nursing care. They have to be registered with both the local authority and the Health Authority (Health Board in Scotland).

The advantage of dual-registered homes is that your relative will not have to move to a different home if her health needs change. There are not many dual-registered homes at present, so you may have difficulty in finding one. This is because the flexibility, which is ideal for the residents, can make budgeting and planning difficult for the home. As a way around this, some dual-registered homes require residents to carry on paying for their room in the 'residential' part of the home while they are temporarily receiving nursing care in the 'nursing' part. If your relative is considering a dual-registered home, you should check their policy on this so that you and your relative are not suddenly faced with an unexpected expense.

For more *i*nformation

ⓘ Counsel and Care Factsheet 4 *Special accommodation for older people.*

ⓘ Contact one of the following organisations. Addresses are listed on pages 84–87.

British Federation of Care Home Proprietors

National Care Homes Association

Registered Nursing Home Association

Independent Healthcare Association

Elderly Accommodation Counsel Has a national database on private and voluntary care homes, and will give you a computer print-out of accommodation in the area and price range you are looking at, and of homes which will accept people with dementia. (It requests a £5 donation towards costs, except from people on a low income.)

ⓘ There is more information about organisations which can help you find a home and useful books and leaflets on pages 43–44 and page 53.

4 Finding the right care home

Everyone has their own ideas about what is important in a care home. Some people like a quiet, restful atmosphere, others like plenty of activity. Some like to look out on green fields, others like to see people going by. People have different preferences in food, decor, companionship.

Sometimes there is such a range of homes to choose from that picking one can be quite daunting. Equally daunting is the challenge facing families where someone is so dependent that they have difficulty in finding a care home that will accept them at all.

This chapter explains how you can find out about care homes which might be suitable for your relative, and suggests guidelines to help you sort out the good homes from the not so good ones.

Roshan

'He said, "It's all right here, but they shout at you. You just have to get used to it."'

'My sister and I were under pressure to find a care home for Mum after the consultant transferred her from the stroke unit to a geriatric ward. The social worker gave us a list of homes. Of the 20 or so we visited, we found two we really liked. The first home we visited was the one recommended by the consultant. It was a lovely big old house, very clean and efficient – and we came away thinking "not over my dead body". It was the atmosphere of efficient bossiness that put us off. We said we were looking for somewhere on the ground floor. They only had an upstairs vacancy, but they offered to move someone who was settled in a downstairs room so Mum could have her room. We said, "No thanks".

'One so-called "family home" was so immaculate, with nice houseplants and delicate china, it just made us feel uncomfortable. The matron seemed very houseproud and pernickety. Even her husband and daughter called her "matron". But the resident we talked to said it was wonderful – so it just goes to show how people differ.

'Quite a few homes were rather smelly. Once, an elderly man came up to us as we were looking round. He said, "It's all right here, but they shout at you. You just have to get used to it."

'We were quite shocked at the number of homes that agreed to take Mum without even seeing her. Another thing which was disturbing was the way, when we were being shown round, they would knock on the door of someone's room and then go barging in without waiting for a reply. Sometimes they didn't even bother to knock. They seemed to be quite unaware that that room was all that was left of someone's home.

'There was only one home where they actually approached someone in the lounge and asked whether we could see their room. That was one of the two we liked.'

Deciding on priorities

Choosing a care home is a very personal matter – especially as you are choosing not only a place to live but the people you will be spending your life with. Often it is a case of weighing up different positives and negatives against each other: a long way from friends and family, but a friendlier atmosphere; having to share a room, but a beautiful view.

It's vital that you and your relative talk about what is really important to her, and what kind of care home she would be happiest in. If your relative is mentally alert, then her feelings and preferences must have priority – after all, it will be her home. However, many families find themselves in the position of having to choose for someone who is not able to decide for herself.

One way to start the discussion is for everyone involved to 'brainstorm' together. On a large sheet of paper, write down all the things which seem important about a home, in the order they come into your heads. Factors to consider include:

- the level of care your relative needs;
- location (where should the home be?);
- cost (your relative will have to meet the full cost if she has savings over £16,000 – see p 56);
- preferred size of home;
- single or shared rooms;
- shared living areas, toilet facilities;
- wheelchair/walking frame access;
- easy access to ground floor/outside;
- any special needs your relative might have, such as diet or therapy, which must be catered for, or any activities she would like to pursue.

You may want to add other things to your list.

When you have got all the points down, try numbering them in order of importance – for example, is a pleasant view more important than decor and furnishings? Is it more important for your relative to be near the family or to stay in the area where she has been living? Now you can make out a list of your relative's priorities, with the most important ones near the top. A list like this can save you a lot of time, by allowing you to eliminate unsuitable homes over the telephone, without the need for a visit.

When you actually come to looking at homes, you may find your list doesn't always apply. For example, even if you have given decor a low priority, you may find a *very* dreary home makes your relative feel depressed. But a list is still a useful starting point, because it helps you focus your minds on the things that really matter.

41

If your relative is from a minority ethnic or religious group

An older person from a minority ethnic group will often say she would be happier in a care home where she can be with people who share the same culture, where her food preferences and religion will be respected, and where she can speak in her mother tongue. There are a number of care homes in the UK which cater for people from minority ethnic and religious groups. The best way to find out more about them is through your own religious or community network, or ethnic publications, newsletters, etc. The local social services department may also be able to help.

Unfortunately you may find that the nearest care home for your relative's ethnic or religious group is in another town away from friends and family. There is no easy answer to this dilemma – it will be up to you and your relative to decide on your priorities.

Sonia

'My Dad thought of going into the Ukrainian home in Leicester when Mum died. The trouble is, it's a long way from all his friends and family. In the end, he decided to stay put.'

Sharanjit

'My Mum was the only Indian person in the home. She was quite lonely, and she didn't like the food.'

David

'Grandad went into a Jewish home in South London. It was just like a holiday camp. He spent his time nattering with the other residents and playing chess. He had a whale of a time.'

Finding out about suitable care homes in your area

A good starting point is to ask around among family and friends. They may be able to tell you about good homes and ones to avoid. Your doctor may know about homes she or he has visited – but be aware that some doctors have a financial interest in private homes.

You should be able to get a list of residential homes which have been inspected and approved from the **social services department** of your local council – ring social services and ask them to post you one. (Social services departments are called social work departments in Scotland.) The **Health Authority** should give you a list of registered nursing homes. Ask at the hospital, or ring the main number for your health authority and ask who you should speak to. Many residential and nursing homes advertise in local newspapers and in the *Yellow Pages*. You could also contact the local Age Concern office, the Community Health Council or the Citizens Advice Bureau.

In addition, there are a number of national organisations which can help you (addresses on pp 83–88). These include:

Counsel and Care Provides advice for older people and their families about finding and choosing a care home, as well as information about private and voluntary sector care homes they have visited in the London area. Can also advise about charitable grants.

Elderly Accommodation Counsel Maintains a national database on private and voluntary care homes; can provide a computer print-out of accommodation in the area and price range you are looking at. They can also identify homes which will accept people with dementia.

Relatives Association Gives help and advice about standards of care to relatives and friends of older people in care homes.

Association of Charity Officers Has details of some charitable care homes for particular professions or occupations, and may also be able to suggest charities which could help with fees.

The following associations of private owners (addresses on pp 84–87) can give you lists of member care homes in a particular area:

British Federation of Care Home Proprietors

National Care Homes Association

Registered Nursing Home Association

If you have difficulty finding a suitable care home

In some parts of the country there are plenty of care homes to choose from. In other places, there may be very few, and they may have a waiting list or be out of your price range. This means that you and your relative may not have a lot of choice. Someone with severe dementia, or someone who is very frail and needs a great deal of nursing care, may find it particularly hard to find a place.

However desperate you feel, do not be tempted to accept the first place you are offered just because they have a vacancy. If your relative has been assessed by social services as being in need of residential or nursing home care, then it is their responsibility to find a suitable home. So if you and your relative cannot find a suitable home, it may be worth asking for a social services assessment even if your relative has sufficient funds to pay the fees herself.

Placement agencies

In some parts of the country there are private placement agencies which offer information and advice about care homes, including financial advice. It is important to be aware that some agencies work on a commission basis, so the advice they offer may not be impartial. In some cases they may make a charge for information which is freely available elsewhere, not least from your own social services department or from Age Concern, Counsel and Care and the other organisations listed above.

What to look for in a care home

Debbie

'Mum got friendly with a couple whose daughter and son-in-law carried on visiting her. It's such a friendly place.'

Roger

'They didn't treat the residents like people at all – just like so many bodies to be shifted about.'

The best way to find out about care homes is to visit as many as you can. Have a good look around and, if you get the opportunity, ask some of the residents what they think of the home. If your relative lives some distance away from you, you can start by visiting homes in your own area, just so you have some points to compare. This will give you an idea of the variety of different management philosophies and atmospheres.

People who are happy in the care home they have chosen, when asked why they like it, very often say, 'It was the atmosphere'.

It is hard to put one's finger on what makes a good atmosphere as everyone's ideas are different, but the questions below may be relevant.

■ What is the matron or manager like? The matron is the person who sets the standards the rest of the staff work to. Do you and your relative like her? Does she seem the sort of person you could talk to openly if something was bothering you? Do you think her replies would be frank and honest? How much time does she spend at the home?

■ Do the residents seem happy? Are people doing things? Is there a pleasant hum of conversation, or is everybody sitting passively looking at the television?

■ Do the staff seem to treat the residents as equal individuals, with their own wants and needs? Or do they treat them like children to be patronised or, worse still, as a nuisance?

■ What are the decor and furnishings like? Bright and attractive surroundings, a pleasant setting and a clean, fresh smell can all make the difference to residents' morale. But don't be too swayed by the appearance of the home; look out for evidence of good care as well.

■ Is the home a member of the National Care Homes Association or the British Federation of Care Home Proprietors? These organisations do keep an eye on the standards of their members. But bear in mind that they are funded by their members' fees, so they are not entirely independent.

Jenny

'The matron answered all my questions, and she said all the right things ... the trouble is, it was all lies.'

'It was a brand new purpose-built nursing home, one that belongs to one of the big national companies, with a glossy brochure, plants and flowers everywhere, and beautifully decorated. I was most impressed. The matron answered all my questions, and she said all the right things. She said they treated all the residents as individuals, and respected their privacy, and tried to cater for their individual needs. She said the home provided activity and stimulation, and took people on outings. The trouble is, it was all lies.

'What I found was that the matron was hardly ever there. Most of the nurses were from agencies, and they weren't there long enough to get to know the residents. The other staff only worked a few hours a week, and there was a big staff turnover, so no relationships developed between the residents and the people looking after them. The staff spent their spare time sitting together in corners and gossiping, rather than talking to the residents.

'What's more they were virtually unsupervised, and they seemed to have no training. They gave my Mum a scalding hot mug of tea to hold in her arthritic hand, with nothing to put it down on. I saw one staff member making fun of a resident because of the way he walked. Another time I saw two of them come up behind an old lady and lift her from her chair, without saying a word to her. They were just completely uncaring. I was shocked.

'If I was to advise anyone now, I would say, spend some time at the home and watch how the staff interact with the residents. And ask the matron to talk to you about one of the residents – without breaching confidentiality – to tell you about her care plan, and see whether it includes social and emotional care, how it matches her personality. It would give you an idea whether the staff really know the residents and care about them.'

Questions to ask over the phone before you visit

These questions may help you eliminate homes which do not meet your relative's needs, and so save you a visit.

- Is the home registered? Is it properly insured and inspected? (If you are looking at a small registered home, with three residents or fewer, there is a chance that it may not have been inspected by the council. It is therefore doubly important that you check thoroughly.)
- Does the home take people with your relative's illness/disability?
- Does it provide the right level of care (for example nursing care if necessary)?
- Is it in a convenient place for you to visit regularly?
- If your relative is in a wheelchair, is there good wheelchair access to all parts of the building?
- Is the building all on one level, or is there an internal lift?
- If your relative needs special treatment or a special diet, will the home be able to provide it?
- What are the fees?
- Can they send you a brochure?
- Is there a suitable vacancy? How long is the waiting list? Is the room single or shared?

Note Even if there is no vacancy at present, you may still wish to visit the home, in order to give you some standards of comparison when looking at other homes.

Questions to ask when you visit

You should not feel awkward about asking a lot of questions. If the home is well run they will respect your concern for your relative. You can read through the list of questions below before you visit and mark the ones which are particularly important. Don't worry if, when you come away, you find you have forgotten to ask something vital – you can always ring up and check. It is more important to be alert and observant when you are looking round.

Questions about how the home is run

■ Are there sufficient trained staff?
■ How long have the staff been there? How many are agency staff?
■ What staff are in the home at night?
■ What arrangements are made to ensure the security of very confused residents? Do these arrangements affect the freedom of movement of residents who are not confused?
■ Is it possible for your relative to stay in the home for a **trial period** of, say, a month or two, to see whether it suits her? (Most homes now offer this.)
■ Is there a **contract** between the care home and the residents? If there is, are you happy about the conditions? Under what circumstances could your relative be asked to leave the home? (See also 'Questions about money matters' below.)
■ What happens if someone has a complaint?
■ What will happen to your relative if her condition deteriorates or improves?
■ What is the home's policy about residents as they approach death? Will your relative be encouraged to stay if her health permits, and given appropriate care and support, or will the home seek to have her admitted to a hospital or hospice?

Questions about privacy and independence

■ Do residents usually look after their own money? What are the arrangements if they are not able to?
■ Do residents have a say about how things are run? Is there a residents' committee?

- Can residents see visitors when and where they choose?
- Is there a telephone they can use for incoming and outgoing calls where they can talk in privacy?
- Do staff knock before going into a resident's room and wait for a reply (unless the resident is deaf)? Can residents have a key to their door?
- Can residents decide for themselves when to go to bed and when to get up in the mornings? If not, are you happy with the arrangements?
- Are they encouraged to do things for themselves and make decisions for themselves as much as possible?
- What happens about clothing and laundry? Do residents always wear their own clothes or are clothes sometimes 'pooled'?

Ahmed

'They used to get them up at four o'clock in the morning, so they could get them washed and breakfasted before the day shift staff came on.'

Questions about the accommodation

- What are the rooms like (ask to see the room that is on offer)?
- If your relative has to share a room, is there any choice about who she shares with?
- Will your relative be able to keep any personal possessions in her room, such as pictures, plants or furniture? Can she decorate the room to her taste?
- Will your relative be able to reach a toilet easily, both from her own room and from the dining room, sitting room and other shared areas?
- Will your relative be able to use the alarm system?
- Is there more than one living room, so that there is a quiet room as well as a television room? Is there an outdoor sitting area?
- What is the policy about smoking? Are there smoking and non-smoking areas?

Questions about doctors and medical matters

- What are the arrangements for handling medicines? Do residents have a say in this?
- Can residents see their own doctor if they want to?
- What are the arrangements for outpatient hospital visits? Will your relative have to pay for transport?
- How much will your relative have to pay if she is in hospital for any length of time?
- Do a chiropodist, dentist and optician visit the home? If not, what arrangements are made? Is chiropody charged as an 'extra' (see pp 51–52)?

Questions about activities

- Are there organised exercise sessions on offer?
- Are there other organised activities residents can get involved in?
- Does the home take residents on trips and visits, for example for shopping, or to the theatre or cinema or to a place of worship?
- Are there up-to-date books, newspapers and magazines for residents?
- Does a mobile library visit, or can residents go to the local library?
- If your relative likes gardening, is there any opportunity for her to be responsible for an area of garden, or perhaps a window box or indoor planter?
- If your relative is used to having a pet, is there a pet in the home she can help look after, or can she take her own pet? The Cinnamon Trust (Tel: 01736 757900) has a list of care homes which allow residents to take their own pets. They may also be able to help with pet care in an emergency.

Kate

'Every morning starts with an exercise session. Then there are different activities. There's an art class on Mondays, which is very popular. Then there's a craft group, a poetry group, and one of the residents leads a musical afternoon.'

Marcus

'Dad's always enjoyed gardening, and one of his pleasures is to go out into the potting shed and plant out the seedlings.'

Derek

'On Sundays Anne goes to the Baptist Church with the proprietor's husband.'

Questions about food and mealtimes

- What is the food like?
- Is there a choice?
- Can residents prepare food and drinks in their own rooms?
- Can they sometimes eat privately with their guests?
- Can residents have a cup of tea or coffee when they want?
- Can residents have an alcoholic drink when they want?
- What is the last meal of the day?
- If your relative has special dietary needs – perhaps ethnic ones – can these be met?

Sue

'They always ask you what you want, and they try to work to your likes and dislikes.'

Questions about money matters

- How much is the weekly fee? What exactly does it cover?
- What are the extras? Ask about hairdressing, chiropody, extra drinks or snacks, special diet, newspapers, a television or telephone in your relative's own room, trips and outings. (Residents or their visitors will usually be expected to buy things for personal use such as clothes, toiletries and stationery,

but some homes cover these as well.) NHS services such as chiropody, incontinence advice, stoma care, and treatments such as physiotherapy or speech therapy should be provided by the health authority or bought in by the local authority if they arranged the care. Incontinence supplies may not always be covered. It is just as well to check who is responsible for paying for these for your relative. (See Age Concern England Factsheet 10 *Local authority charging procedures for residential and nursing home care.*)

■ What opportunities will there be for your relative to spend her personal expenses allowance (see p 57)?

■ What are the arrangements for residents collecting pensions and other income, and paying the fees?

■ Do you have to pay a deposit on booking? Is it refundable?

■ If the home puts up its fees, how much notice do residents get?

■ If your relative is away from the home for a short time, for example in hospital, or on holiday or staying with other family members, what fees will she still have to pay?

■ Is there a contract to sign? Who has to sign it – the person staying in the home or another family member? (If you are asked to sign a contract on behalf of your relative, you should seek legal advice from a solicitor or the Citizens Advice Bureau about what exactly you are committing yourself to.)

■ What happens to a self-funding resident if her savings run out and the fees are above the level the social services department is willing to pay?

■ How much notice will you have to give if your relative leaves the home (for example to go and live with a family member, or to go into a different home that provides a higher level of care)?

■ What happens about payment if your relative dies while she is in the home?

Things to look out for when you visit

■ Is the home clean? Does it smell fresh?

■ Is it homely? Are there plants and flowers around?

■ Is the atmosphere busy and friendly?

■ How do the staff behave towards the residents? Do they seem rude, brisk, patronising, impatient, treat them like children?

■ Are the other residents the sort of people your relative could get on with and make friends with? Or are all the other residents much older and/or more physically or mentally disabled than your relative?

Liz

'The husband of one of the staff members has this motorbike, which he's built up himself from parts. She always used to tell the residents about how he was working on it. One day, when it was finished, he brought it round to show everyone, and all the residents had a go sitting on it and had their photos taken.'

For more *information*

ℹ Age Concern England Factsheet 29 *Finding residential and nursing home accommodation.*

ℹ Counsel and Care Factsheet 5 *What to look for in a private or voluntary registered home.*

ℹ Counsel and Care Factsheet 13 *Finding suitable residential and nursing home accommodation* (London only).

ℹ Carers National Association Factsheet 4a *Finding, choosing and paying for residential care.*

ℹ Help the Aged Information Sheet 10 *Residential and nursing homes.*

ℹ *A Better Home Life: A code of good practice for residential and nursing home care,* published by the Centre for Policy on Ageing (0171–253 1787).

ℹ Your local social services department has to make public their inspection reports on the homes registered with them. Ask your social worker or contact the Inspection Unit to find out where these can be seen. Contact the Health Authority to find out if their inspection reports can be seen.

5 Paying for a care home

Residential and nursing homes can be very expensive. While some people pay the full fees themselves, people with income and savings below a certain amount may get help with the cost.

Under the 1990 NHS and Community Care Act (which came fully into force in April 1993), anyone who needs help towards the cost of paying for residential or nursing home care must first be assessed by their local social services department to see whether they need to be in a care home. If they need such care, they will be assessed to see how much they should pay towards the cost. Most people who were permanently in a private or voluntary care home before April 1993 are not affected.

The rules for working out who should pay what are quite complicated. This chapter explains how your relative's contribution will be assessed. It also looks at what you can do if your relative can no longer manage her own affairs.

Oleg

'The social worker said they could have helped Dad with the cost right from the start.'

'The doctor at the hospital said that with good nursing care Dad should be walking about within a few weeks, so we thought his stay in the home would only be temporary. Well, he had £4,000 left from his retirement lump sum and a reasonable pension, so he told us not to bother with social services, and to use his savings to pay the fees of the home. But the fees were £398 a week, and after a couple of months his savings were down to half. I had no idea they would disappear so fast. Although he could walk again, he found it very hard to get up out of his chair without help, because his muscles were so wasted. We realised there was no way he could go back to living on his own. We would have to do something fast, but we had no idea what to do. We rang up the hospital, and they told us to contact social services. The social worker said they could have helped Dad with the cost of the home right from the start.'

The social services means test

If your relative wishes to enter a residential or nursing home and needs help to pay the fees, she will have to have her care needs assessed by the social services department, as explained on pages 12–16. If they decide to arrange a place for her, they will then be responsible for meeting the full cost of the care home, but they will assess your relative to see how much she should pay towards the cost. This is called a **means test** or **financial assessment**, and it is carried out according to national rules set by the Government.

Social services will *either* pay the care home themselves and then collect your relative's contribution from her *or* – if both your relative and the care home owner agree – they will ask her to pay the assessed amount direct to the home and pay the balance themselves.

Even if your relative is initially going to pay the full fees of the care home herself, it is a good idea to ask the social services department for an assessment of her needs. If her savings drop to £16,000 while she is still living in the home, she will be able – and may have – to turn to social services for help with paying the fees. If they do not think that she needs to be in a care home at all, or if she is in a nursing home whereas they think she only needs to be in a residential home, then they may refuse to pay all or part of the fees.

55

Savings and investments

The local authority means test is very similar but not identical to the Department of Social Security means test for Income Support. Someone who has savings or investments above £16,000 will have to pay the full cost of a care home. If savings are held in joint names, then half of their value will be counted. If your relative owns her own **house** or **flat**, its value could be counted as part of her savings. However, there are exceptions. For more on what happens to your relative's own home see pages 61–63.

Even if your relative starts by paying the full cost of the care home, don't forget to apply to the council at once when her savings start to drop down towards £16,000. This could happen quite quickly. Don't wait until she has no savings left at all.

If your relative has savings between £10,000 and £16,000 they are counted as adding to her income (see below for how income is assessed). Each £250 or part of £250 above £10,000 is counted as £1 per week income. Savings below £10,000 do not count.

Deprivation of assets

Some people try to get around the savings rule by giving money or property away to family members. This is called deprivation of assets. If this happens within six months of the person going into a care home and the person needs help with funding from the local authority, and the local authority thinks that it has been done deliberately to avoid having to use the savings or assets to pay for care, then they can get the money back from the people it was given to.

Even if the transfer took place longer than six months before, they can assess the person as if they still had the capital. But they do have to prove that the intention was to avoid paying the care home fees, or to pay less.

Income

If your relative's weekly income is more than the cost of the home, then she will obviously be able to pay the full amount herself. But if her income is less, and her savings are no more than £16,000, then the local authority should make up the difference.

To work out how much help a person should get with the cost of the care home, the local authority adds together all their weekly income and subtracts it from the weekly fees of the home – although some types of income, such as the mobility component of Disability Living Allowance (see p 65), are ignored. They then pay the balance. (If your relative wants to go into a more expensive home than the council is willing to pay for, see pp 59–60.)

The person is allowed a small **personal expenses allowance** (£14.45 in 1998), which is hers to spend as she chooses, for example on clothes, personal gifts, toiletries or little luxuries.

The local authority will probably check that your relative is receiving all the State benefits to which she is entitled, including the State Retirement Pension and Income Support. These benefits will be taken into account by the local authority.

Claiming Income Support

Income Support is a benefit for people whose income is below what the Government thinks they need to live on. Pensioners and sick and disabled people get extra amounts known as **premiums**. If your relative is entering a private or voluntary care home and her income is below this level and her savings are no more than £16,000, she will be able to claim Income Support (including any premiums that she qualifies for) plus **residential allowance**, which is paid as part of Income Support to help with the housing costs of care in a residential or nursing home (there is a slightly higher rate for people living in Greater London).

The £16,000 capital rule only applies if your relative enters a home on a permanent basis. If she is a temporary resident then the capital rule is £8,000 until she becomes permanent. This is for Income Support only. The £16,000 capital limits apply to both temporary and permanent residents in the local authority assessment.

Certain sorts of income are ignored or 'disregarded', including:

- actual income on savings between £10,000 and £16,000, for which £1 per £250 or part of £250 will already have been counted;
- Attendance Allowance or Disability Living Allowance;
- any money from a relative or charity to pay for extras such as hairdressing or special outings which are not included in the fees of the care home.

Unlike with ordinary Income Support, the Department of Social Security will only take into account the income and savings of the person who is going into a care home, not their partner's. If someone is applying for Income Support for a **temporary** stay in a care home (up to 52 weeks), then their spouse's income can be taken into account.

Someone going into a local authority home can claim Income Support only if their income is less than the State Retirement Pension. They cannot claim residential allowance. But it does not make a lot of difference to the person going into the home, as all their income (apart from their personal expenses allowance) must go towards the cost of the home anyway.

Helen

'When I was in hospital I talked to other women who told me about the places they'd visited and the holidays they'd been on. And all I'd done was work and work, and save and save, so that my daughters could have something when I died. But when they did the assessment, I was told I would have to spend all the money I'd saved before I could get any help with paying for the home. I realise now I made a big mistake.'

For more *i*nformation

❶ Age Concern England Factsheet 10 *Local authority charging procedures for residential and nursing home care.*

❶ Age Concern England Factsheet 25 *Income Support and the Social Fund.*

ⓘ Counsel and Care Factsheet 19 *Paying the fees of a registered private or voluntary home for people who entered the home on or after 1st April 1993.*

ⓘ Age Concern England Factsheet 38 *Treatment of the former home as capital for people in residential and nursing homes.*

ⓘ Age Concern England Factsheet 39 *Paying for care in a residential or nursing home if you have a partner.*

ⓘ Age Concern England Factsheet 40 *Transfer of assets and paying for care in a residential or nursing home.*

ⓘ *Your Rights*, published annually by Age Concern Books (details on p 91), a comprehensive guide to money benefits for older people.

If your relative chooses a more expensive home

The social services department should have a list of private and voluntary homes which it has approved. If your relative wants to go into a more expensive home than the council would usually pay for for someone with your relative's assessed needs, you or another family member can make up the difference, provided that the council agrees. The council will enter into a separate contract with you for the 'top-up' amount, as it will be legally liable for the whole fee.

If at some future date you and your family cannot afford to pay the 'top-up' amount, you may be able to get help from a charity. There are hundreds of charities in Britain. Some are large national charities which have become household names; others are small charities set up to help particular groups of people, for example people who have worked in a certain industry or occupation. The best way to find out whether there is a charity which could help your relative is to write to the Association of Charity Officers or contact Charity Search (addresses on pp 83 and 84).

But if there is no place available at what the council says is its 'usual' amount, *they* must fund the difference. Government guidance states that local authorities cannot set arbitrary ceilings on the amount they will pay. They must pay the full cost of meeting assessed needs.

If you do not feel that the place your relative is offered meets her needs – for example for a single room or to be near her spouse or family – you should say so and ask for her case to be looked at again.

If your relative wants to move to a home in a different area

It sometimes happens that an older person chooses to go into a care home that is not in the area where they live, perhaps to be near their family. There should be no problem about this, and the social services department in their own area will generally agree to pay the cost of the home. If the home costs more than they are willing to pay, the family can 'top up' the amount as described above, so long as the local authority agrees.

So who pays what?

Your relative pays ALL her income except a small personal expenses allowance, which she is allowed to keep.

The Department of Social Security (DSS) pays Income Support, including residential allowance.

The local authority pays the amount it has agreed.

You or other family members pay any difference between what the local authority has agreed and the actual cost of the home.

However, the local authority has legal responsibility for paying the fees, and will have a contract with the care home if it is not run by them. They must collect any contributions from your relative and other family members.

For more *i*nformation

i Age Concern England Factsheet 10 *Local authority charging procedures for residential or nursing home care.*

i For extra help and advice, contact your nearest **Citizens Advice Bureau** or the local **Age Concern** group.

What happens to your relative's own home?

Someone going into a care home can usually have a **trial period** first, to see whether she is going to be happy there. Most local authorities allow a trial period of up to six weeks. During this time, it is important that your relative keeps her options open, and doesn't give up or sell her own home.

If she rents her home

If your relative is renting her home, and there is no one else living there, then she will probably have to give up the tenancy once she moves permanently into a care home.

In some cases, especially with council houses or flats, it may be possible to assign the tenancy to another member of the family who has been living there. This depends on the policy of the local authority. Your relative should speak to the housing manager if she would like to do this.

If she is renting from a private landlord, her rights will depend on how long she has been in the property and what kind of tenancy she has. In this situation, it is best to get advice from a solicitor or a Citizens Advice Bureau.

If she owns her home

If your relative owns her own home, then its value is counted as part of her savings and capital. But this does not apply if her stay in a care home is only going to be temporary (up to 52 weeks). If her stay is going to be permanent, its value will be counted as part of her savings. This will almost always come to more than £16,000, which means that she will have to pay the full cost of the care home herself until her savings have dropped down to £16,000.

Most people arrange for their property to be sold. If your relative's home is on the market, its value will not affect her entitlement to Income Support for at least the first six months. However, it will affect the local authority's assessment of what she should pay right from the start, and they will assess her as having capital (the value of the property less a notional 10 per cent for the expenses of selling). Once the property is sold her capital will be the net value of the sale less costs.

Although your relative cannot be forced to sell her home to pay for residential or nursing home care, if she chooses not to sell then the local authority can put a **charge** on it. This means that when the property is eventually sold they have first claim on the proceeds to pay off the money she owes them.

Some local authorities are now refusing to make the arrangements for people who have a house to sell as they are considered to have over £16,000. This sometimes causes difficulties as it may take time before the capital can be realised. The Department of Health has stated that it 'would not condone the practice of advising or recommending residents to obtain a commercial loan'. You may wish to seek advice if you would have difficulties in meeting the fees or use the local authority complaints procedure if you feel the local authority should have arranged your care and helped with the funding whilst the house was for sale.

The value of your relative's home may not be counted as part of her savings and capital if there is someone else living in it who is:

■ a spouse or partner;

■ another relative who is aged 60 or over or disabled (see Age Concern England Factsheet 10 *Local authority charging procedures for residential or nursing home care* for who is counted as a 'relative' or 'disabled').

If there is someone else living in your relative's home who does not fall into one of these categories, the value of the home could still be completely ignored at the discretion of the local authority. This could be:

■ an older person (60 or over) who is not a relative;

■ a younger person who has given up their own home to live with your relative and care for her.

If you think this could apply in your relative's case, it is a good idea to get advice from Age Concern England or a Citizens Advice Bureau. You may have to use the complaints procedure to have this looked at again.

For more *i*nformation

ℹ Age Concern England Factsheet 38 *Treatment of the former home as capital for people in residential and nursing homes.*

Can anyone else be asked to pay the cost of care for your relative?

In some situations, a person's spouse can be asked to contribute towards the cost of their care because they are classed as a **liable relative**. (An unmarried partner has no liability to pay for a partner's care.) Usually, payment is voluntary and the social services department will try to agree a fair amount with the spouse, but they can apply for a court order if they think the husband or wife can afford to pay something but is refusing to do so. Only a court can rule how much, if anything, a spouse should contribute.

When carrying out the means test, the local authority can only take into account the savings and income of the person who is going into the care home, not their spouse's. Where savings or assets are held in joint names, it will be assumed that half belongs to each partner. A spouse is *not* obliged to give financial details as part of the social services financial assessment, and the use of a joint assessment form is inappropriate. In reaching a voluntary agreement with the local authority, it is likely that spouses will need to give information about their income and assets, but the Department of Health has advised local authorities that their expenditure and standard of living should be taken into account – there are no national rules about what contribution a spouse should make.

No other family members – children, grandchildren, brothers or sisters – can be made to contribute to the cost of a relative's care, although they can choose to do so. Family members may, however, pay for 'extras' such as hairdressing or special outings which are not included in the fees of the home (see pp 51–52). Essential health services such as specialist nursing, physiotherapy and continence advice should not be classed as 'extras' and should be paid for by the health authority when the local authority is making the arrangement.

For more *i*nformation

ⓘ Age Concern England Factsheet 39 *Paying for care in a residential or nursing home if you have a partner.*

What happens if spouses' incomes are very unequal?

Where someone going into a care home receives an occupational pension or other income in their own name, this is fully taken into account in the local authority means test. This can mean that the income of the spouse who continues to live at home is greatly reduced, causing real hardship – for example where a couple's main source of income is the husband's occupational pension and the wife has very little income of her own.

Changes were made to the regulations in 1996 and 1997. The situation is now that the local authority will disregard (ignore) 50 per cent of an occupational or personal pension or payment from a retirement annuity contract if it is being passed over to a spouse. The spouse must not be living in the same care home as the resident. It does not apply to unmarried couples. For more details of the rules see Factsheet 39 *Paying for care in a residential or nursing home if you have a partner.*

People who were in homes before April 1993

Special rules apply to people who were permanently in a registered private or voluntary care home before April 1993. These rules are explained in Age Concern England Factsheet 11 *Financial support for people in residential and nursing homes prior to 1 April 1993.*

Attendance Allowance or Disability Living Allowance in a care home

If your relative pays the full fees of a private or voluntary care home herself, then she can claim – or continue to be paid – Attendance Allowance or Disability Living Allowance (DLA) provided she fulfils the other conditions.

Attendance Allowance is a weekly allowance paid to someone over the age of 65 who becomes ill or disabled. It is paid at two rates, according to how much care the person needs.

DLA is for people who become ill or disabled before the age of 65. The **care component** is paid at three levels.

If your relative needs local authority help with the care home fees, or enters a council-run home, she cannot start to receive Attendance Allowance or the care component of DLA. If she is already receiving one of these allowances, it will stop four weeks after she enters the home, unless the arrangements have been made without social services being involved (see below).

The **mobility component** of DLA is paid at three different levels. It can normally be claimed or continue to be paid regardless of whether a person lives in a private, voluntary or local authority home.

Housing Benefit and Council Tax Benefit in a care home

Someone going into a care home cannot usually claim Housing Benefit, but there are exceptions, including some Abbeyfield homes, Royal Charter or Act of Parliament homes, or local authority homes which do not provide board. If you think your relative could benefit, you should ask for more information (see below).

People in residential or nursing homes do not usually have to pay Council Tax.

Making your own arrangements

Some people may choose to make their own arrangements without involving social services at all. In this case they may be able to continue claiming Attendance Allowance or Disability Living Allowance even though they are getting Income Support (if social services make the arrangement the allowance stops after four weeks).

Someone whose income and savings are below Income Support level, and who has made arrangements without involving social services, may be able to put together a package consisting of:

65

- State Pension and occupational pension (if any);
- Attendance Allowance or Disability Living Allowance;
- Income Support (including any premiums) plus residential allowance.

This may be enough, or almost enough, to pay for their care, depending on the fees of the home.

When the rules about qualifying for these benefits were made, it was not intended that people could claim Income Support and still receive Attendance Allowance or Disability Living Allowance. Because the rules are quite complicated, and because the rules may change, it is best to check with Age Concern England or Counsel and Care (addresses on pp 89 and 85) if you want to use this provision.

Someone paying for herself and not claiming Income Support can claim Attendance Allowance or Disability Living Allowance whether or not social services have been involved. Your relative may find that her pension, occupational pension, other income and Attendance Allowance will add up to cover the cost of the fees, with maybe just a small 'top-up' from her family or her own savings.

However, if your relative has to dip into her savings too much, she might find herself running out of funds. If this seems possible, then she should contact social services at an early stage and go through the assessment procedure.

Although some people may prefer not to involve social services at all, it is still possible to get this package of benefits as long as the social services department does not have a contract with the home for you individually. You could therefore have an assessment and still decide to arrange your own care. The people who get the most advantage from using this package of benefits are those who have houses to sell.

Age Concern explains this subject in more detail in its leaflet *Paying for residential and nursing home fees from income support and attendance allowance*. It is best to check with Age Concern England before using this provision.

For more information

ⓘ Age Concern England Factsheet 10 *Local authority charging procedures for residential and nursing home care.*

ⓘ Age Concern England Factsheet 18 *A brief guide to money benefits.*

ⓘ *Your Rights*, published annually by Age Concern Books (details on p 91), an excellent guide to money benefits for older people.

ⓘ Ask at your local **Citizens Advice Bureau** or other advice centre. If necessary, they can help people make a claim.

Managing your relative's money

If your relative is too physically disabled or mentally frail to manage alone, you may need to think about becoming involved in or taking over the running of her affairs.

Collecting her State Pension and other benefits

If your relative is still mentally competent – that is, capable of understanding what she is doing – she can nominate you or another relative to collect her State Pension and any other benefits, including Income Support, from the post office as her agent. Alternatively, she could arrange to have them paid direct into a bank or building society account.

If she is not capable of understanding what she is doing, telephone the local Benefits Agency (social security) office and say that you or another close relative would like to become the **appointee** to collect benefits on her behalf. If you and the rest of the family live too far away, then the local Benefits Agency office may recommend someone, or a local voluntary agency such as Age Concern may be able to find an advocate who will become the appointee. As a 'last resort', if no one else can be found, the person in charge of the care home may be appointed – if this happens, the benefits office must inform the Registration and Inspection Unit.

67

Using bank and building society accounts

If your relative is mentally competent, she may authorise you to use her bank or building society account. This is known as a 'third party mandate'.

Power of attorney

In England and Wales, this is a document which gives someone the legal right to manage the affairs of another person – your relative might, for example, want you to sell her home for her after she has moved into a care home.

An **ordinary power of attorney** only applies so long as the person giving it is mentally capable and can give instructions to the person who is acting as their 'attorney'. You can get a form to create a power of attorney from a legal stationer, or you can ask a solicitor to help you.

Your relative should not choose anyone connected with the care home as attorney, as this lays open the possibility of financial abuse.

If your relative seems to be getting more forgetful and absent-minded, and you are worried that she may soon become incapable of managing her affairs or suffer from dementia, then it is a good idea for her to create an **enduring power of attorney**. This remains valid even if the person giving it later becomes mentally incapable. But the person giving it must be capable of understanding the nature and effect of creating an enduring power at the time they give it.

This is not an easy subject to discuss and many people avoid it until it is too late. One option is to draw up an enduring power of attorney that will come into effect only under certain conditions, for example if your relative's doctor diagnoses her as having dementia. Sometimes people discuss these conditions and make arrangements at the same time as making their Will, as part of preparing for the future. If your relative has not made a Will, try to encourage her to do so.

As soon as you believe that your relative is becoming or has become mentally disordered and can no longer manage her affairs, you must register the enduring power of attorney with the Public Trust Office (address on p 85).

Applying to the Court of Protection

In England and Wales, if your relative becomes mentally incapable and she has not created an enduring power of attorney, you may need to apply to the Court of Protection for authorisation to manage her finances for her. If she has assets of more than £5,000 the Court will usually appoint and supervise a **receiver** to manage her affairs. Where her savings are less than £5,000 or her affairs are very straightforward, the Court may issue a **short order** or **directions** authorising you to use her assets for her benefit in a certain way.

Applying to the Court of Protection is expensive and complicated, and it is better to avoid it if you can by encouraging your relative to create an enduring power of attorney in good time.

For more *i*nformation

ℹ *Enduring Power of Attorney* and *Handbook for Receivers*, available free of charge from the Court of Protection. Send a large sae to the address on page 85.

ℹ Age Concern England Factsheet 22 *Legal arrangements for managing financial affairs.*

ℹ *Managing Other People's Money*, published by Age Concern Books (details on p 91).

ℹ To find out more about the **Court of Protection**, or to make an application, contact the address on page 85. You may also find it helpful to speak to a Citizens Advice Bureau or see a solicitor.

Managing someone else's affairs in Scotland

Informal arrangements

A legal principle (called **negotiorum gestio**) allows you to act on behalf of an incapable person, provided your actions are for her benefit. It applies when it can be assumed that the person would have authorised you if she had been capable. This principle may be useful in an emergency situation, for example when immediate repairs are required to a house and you need to claim back money spent on someone else's behalf. Some organisations may not accept this informal arrangement.

Power of attorney

If the power of attorney was signed after 1 January 1991 it will remain valid after the person giving it becomes mentally incapable. A solicitor will be needed to prepare the power of attorney.

Curator bonis

If your relative has not appointed a power of attorney and is mentally incapable of looking after her affairs or appointing someone else to look after them, then a **curator bonis** may have to be appointed. A curator bonis is an individual appointed by and responsible to the court. Usually a solicitor or accountant is appointed (though not necessarily) and the curator has to manage all the financial affairs and property of the person. The application to the court for a curator bonis to be appointed is prepared by a solicitor, usually on behalf of a close relative of the person. Having a curator appointed is expensive and any professional will charge an annual administration fee. It is therefore not recommended for people with less than £15,000 of capital.

For more *i*nformation

ⓘ *Dementia: Money and Legal Matters*, available free to carers from Alzheimer Scotland – Action on Dementia (address on p 83).

ⓘ Age Concern Factsheet 22 *Legal arrangements for managing financial affairs* available from Age Concern Scotland (address on p 89).

ⓘ *Information for Families of Persons subject to Curatory*, leaflet available free from the Accountant of Court, 2 Parliament House, Parliament Square, Edinburgh EH1 1RQ.

ⓘ *Dementia in the Community*, leaflet available free from the Mental Welfare Commission for Scotland, K Floor, Argyle House, 3 Lady Lawson Street, Edinburgh EH3 9SH.

6 Staying involved

Once your relative is settled into her care home, your relationship with her will inevitably change. Many people talk about the relief and peace of mind they feel knowing that their relative is well looked after. For others, there is continued anxiety about her well-being, maybe even confrontation with the staff at the home. In some cases, you may find yourself having to help her move to another home. What ever your experience, your continued involvement is as important as ever.

This chapter looks at the various ways in which you may continue to be involved in your relative's life.

Kathy

'Mother was often left on her own for long periods of time ... Sometimes I think they disconnected the buzzer on purpose.'

Kathy's mother had a tumour on her spine. Despite a series of operations, it recurred. Although she was managing well at home and could walk with a zimmer frame, the doctor told her that she would eventually need full-time nursing care, so she decided to sell up and move into a nursing home. Kathy and her sister helped her look at a number of homes. They felt they were lucky to find a home in the village close to where her sister lived.

'It was all brand new, custom-built and beautifully furnished, and all on one floor, so there would be no problem with a wheelchair. It seemed perfect.

'Mother was almost blind and was getting deaf, and we knew she was also going to become increasingly paralysed, so it was very important that the home would give her plenty of stimulation. Well, that's what they promised us, but the reality was very different. We found the owner was running the home as a sideline to his main business, which was hosiery. The staff were never there long – they kept changing. Some of them were lads who just messed about.

'Mother was often left on her own for long periods of time. She had to buzz every time she needed something. Sometimes I think they disconnected her buzzer on purpose. When that happened, she had to telephone one of us at home, and we would then have to get through to the home by telephone, just to get them to walk two yards up the corridor to her room.

'She had no quality of life at all. Sometimes when we went round her hearing aid was lying on the floor, and she couldn't reach down to pick it up. They often forgot to clean her teeth in the morning. She got bedsores, because they didn't turn her often enough.

'My sister and I did complain once or twice. They were always very nice to our faces, but then the matron sent this very formal, legalistic letter, more or less implying that if mother didn't stop complaining (which they said was upsetting the other residents) she would have to leave.

'We felt helpless really. We thought of moving her to a different home, but by then she needed so much care that we thought we'd have trouble finding another home that would take her on. Besides, we didn't think she had that much longer to live. We didn't want to have all the upset and upheaval of moving her when she was so near the end. We wanted her to have a bit of peace and dignity. It sounds awful to say this, but it came as a relief when she died.'

Keeping an eye on the quality of care

Your relative's care plan

In most homes, once your relative has settled in, the matron will draw up a 'care plan' detailing the regular care she will receive, including medication, personal care, any special diet or treatments, and nursing care if appropriate.

Most social services departments encourage homes registered with them to draw up their own care plan for each resident. This should cover needs identified in the care plan drawn up by the social services department when they do their assessment, but may be more detailed or include additional needs identified by the care home manager.

You can help your relative by making sure the home knows about any special needs she may have, so they can be included in the care plan, and by checking that she is getting the care.

Practical ways of keeping an eye on things

There are practical ways you can keep an eye on the quality of care your relative is getting. The following checklist will help warn you of the **danger signs** if something is going seriously wrong.

Physical neglect

If your relative can't look after herself, is she clean and tidy? Have her hair and fingernails been trimmed? Is she wearing clean and appropriate clothing? Does she seem to be getting enough to eat?

Jenny

'Mum's hair and nails were long, and she had an awful bruise on her cheek. I asked the nurse how she'd got the bruise, and she said, "I don't know". They were fed and kept clean, and that's all.'

73

Poor hygiene

Is your relative's bedding clean and dry? Does her room smell fresh and clean? If she has an 'accident' how long does she have to wait for a change of clothing or bedding?

Emotional neglect

Does your relative ever seem bewildered or upset? If she is not able to speak for herself, can the staff give you a reasonable explanation of what has gone wrong? Or do they 'blame' her and say she is being 'difficult'? Has there been any unpleasant incident? (Sometimes other residents are able to shed light on something that has happened, such as a disagreement with a member of staff.)

Jenny

'Once my Dad went round at bath-time, and he heard her screaming. There were three of them – two were holding her and the other was washing her. I raised this with the staff and was told, "Oh, she's awful to bath". I said she shouldn't be forced if she was upset, and I suggested they change the bath-time to the morning, when she's not so tired. They agreed. But next time we went we saw nothing had changed.'

Poor supervision

Has your relative had an accident or been at risk of an accident? Does she have any unexplained cuts or bruises?

Problems with medication

Who supervises the administering of drugs and medicines? Is the person mature and competent? When did your relative last see a doctor?

(It is always better if your relative can keep her own GP, but this may not be possible. If you have any doubts about her medication, try to speak to the doctor who prescribed it.)

Unnecessary sedation

Is your relative receiving sedative drugs to control her behaviour? Who determines the dose? (Sometimes a prescription allows staff in a home to increase the dose if they think it is necessary.) Does your relative seem unduly drowsy or passive or absent-minded? Based on your experience of her, do you think sedation is necessary? Has she been difficult or aggressive before, or has she become so since moving into the care home? (Sometimes homes use sedation as an easy way of dealing with a resident's feelings of distress and dislocation, rather than listening and talking and helping her to settle.) If you have any worries about sedatives, speak to the doctor who prescribed them, and check whether it is really necessary and whether she is getting the right dose.

Undue restraint

Older people who are confused or suffer from dementia do tend to wander, and can put themselves and others at risk, so there has to be some restriction on their movement. However, they should not be prisoners. Drawing the line between safety and undue restraint is always difficult, and each home will set its own rules, which should largely reflect the needs of the residents.

In general, doors should not be locked unless a care home is near a busy main road or other source of danger, but some homes do have double catches or ones which are awkward to open, so that confused residents cannot simply wander out. Residents should never be locked into their own rooms.

While a chair with a table across it may be useful for drinks, snacks or activities, it should be easily movable, and residents should not be forced to sit all day – they should be free to get up and move around. Nor should residents be strapped into chairs unless they have a condition which makes them physically in danger of falling.

Boredom

Mind-numbing boredom can cause misery even in seemingly well-run homes. This is especially a problem where disabled residents

75

rely on staff for company and stimulation. Are the staff spending enough time with residents? Is there a variety of activities including trips and outings? These are so often promised in brochures, but they are one of the first corners to be cut if staff are short on the ground.

Unpleasant behaviour of other residents

It sometimes happens that residents who are abusive or aggressive can turn on other residents in the home and make their lives a misery. If this happens, it is really a case of poor supervision – staff should be aware of what is happening and step in *before* any unpleasantness.

Financial abuse

There have been cases where staff in homes have stolen residents' money or possessions. At the same time, it is a very common sign of dementia that people mislay things then accuse others of stealing them.

Your relative should have a regular weekly personal expenses allowance (see p 57), which is hers to spend as she chooses. If this seems to be disappearing faster than it should, you should mention it to the matron. One answer might be for your relative to have a locking drawer or safe box where she can keep money and valuables. (But if she is inclined to be forgetful, it is a good idea for you to ask her for a spare key.) Government guidance recommends that all homes should have a safe or secure locked storage place and that residents should be given receipts for all valuables and money deposited there.

With larger sums of money, there is greater scope for abuse. The proprietor and staff at the home should not act as agents for the residents, or get involved in their financial affairs, or accept gifts or gratuities. No one connected with the home should ever have a power of attorney or enduring power of attorney (see p 68) over your relative's affairs. If you or another family member cannot take on this role, the Court of Protection will usually appoint a receiver to handle your relative's finances (see p 69).

Making a complaint

If you have doubts or worries about your relative's care, and you're not sure whether they are reasonable, try talking it over with a professional such as a social worker or your relative's GP. Or contact the **Relatives Association** (address on p 87). They will help you decide whether to make a complaint. But before you make a formal complaint it is better to try and clear the matter up with the matron or other staff in the home.

Residents in a home are very vulnerable to abuse, and the staff have a lot of power in relation to them. So residents and their families are often reluctant to complain when things go wrong because they are afraid that they will be victimised. These fears may be justified – no one likes to be criticised – but there are ways of making your point without putting the staff's backs up. It's not so much what you say as how you say it. The following suggestions may help:

- Don't speak out while you're feeling very angry or upset. Wait until you've calmed down a bit and can think clearly about what you want to say.
- Don't criticise. Make practical suggestions for how you would like things to be.
- Don't accuse. Assume that staff mean well and want to put things right.
- Do show understanding of the staff's situation.
- Don't blame. Do encourage good practice.
- Do remember that the reason for speaking out is to get things changed – not to make you feel better.

Making a formal complaint

Should you feel you are getting nowhere, then you or your relative can make a formal complaint. Each home must have a complaints procedure, which should be set out in the brochure or handbook. If you are not sure, ask the person in charge what the complaints procedure is. If you feel nervous about doing this, remember that the procedure is there to offer protection and to help problems be resolved in a friendly way.

If your complaint is ignored, then you can make a formal complaint to the registering authority. Complaints about nursing homes should be made to the Health Authority (Health Board in Scotland). Ask for the department which registers and inspects nursing homes. Complaints about residential homes should be reported to the Inspection or Registration Unit at the local social services department. You can ask for your complaint to be kept confidential.

It is important for people to complain if they are unhappy about the way a home is run, so that abuse and bad practice can be brought out into the open.

It is unusual for a home to be deregistered, but it may happen that a home is threatened with deregistration unless certain changes are made. It is more likely that the social services department will make recommendations or suggest better staff training. In either case, your complaint will help not only your relative but also others living in the home who may not have anyone to speak up for them.

The Relatives Association (address on p 87) or the local Age Concern group may help you and back you up in your complaint.

If the home is a member of one of the national bodies such as the National Care Homes Association or the British Federation of Care Home Proprietors (addresses on pp 87 and 84), you can also contact them directly. They may ask the proprietor to make changes.

If your complaint is very serious, or if your complaint is about the social services department, your local councillor may take up your case or help you to contact the Local Government Ombudsman (address on p 86), who looks into cases of maladministration by local authorities that cause injustice.

Moving to a different home

There are a number of reasons why someone might want to move to a different home. Some of the more common reasons are:

Unhappiness

If your relative is not happy, and does not like the home or the people who look after her, she might be happier somewhere else. It is a good idea to try the informal and formal complaints procedures outlined above. But if this fails, you may decide to look for a more suitable home (see Chapter 4).

Changing care needs

At some point in the future your relative may need a higher level of care than the home can provide. If she is in a residential home, she may need to move to a nursing home. In this case, you should contact the social services department and ask for her care needs to be reassessed. Because a nursing home is usually more expensive, social services will not be willing to arrange nursing home care for your relative unless she has been assessed as needing nursing care. Social services should also help you to find a suitable place.

Equally, if your relative is in a nursing home but her condition is now so improved that she could manage in a residential home, where she would have more freedom and independence, then you can contact the social services department to ask for a reassessment and help in finding a suitable place. She may even be able to consider moving out of a care home, perhaps to live with a member of the family.

Family reasons

Sometimes an older person in a care home may choose to move nearer to her family, to make it easier for them to visit. If she has been getting help with fees from the local social services department, then they should carry on paying for her. Once you have found a home that you and your relative are happy with, approach the social services department in the area where your relative lives at present and explain that she would like to transfer. If the home is more expensive than they are willing to pay for, you or your family may have to 'top up' the fees, as explained on pages 59–60. But beware of falling into the trap described below.

Financial reasons

Someone who is in a more expensive care home than the local authority is willing to pay for may need to move if their family can no longer afford to 'top up' their fees. Or someone who has been paying their own fees may need to move if their money has run out and the social services department will not meet the fees of the home they are in. In either case, the person may have to go to a cheaper home.

Another option might be to stay in the same home but share a room. This can be quite upsetting for someone who has been used to a certain level of comfort and privacy. It is best to avoid this situation by being very careful to choose a home which you think you and your relative will be able to afford for the foreseeable future. But of course it is not always possible to predict what will happen. Contact the Association of Charity Officers or Charity Search (addresses on pp 83 and 84) to find out about charities that might be able to help you.

Note **Whatever your relative's reasons for moving to a new home, it is important to make sure that she gives sufficient notice to the home she is leaving. Otherwise she may find herself paying out two sets of care home fees, which could be extremely expensive. She may have to do this anyway if the new home won't hold the vacancy.**

Positive involvement

This chapter has looked at some of the problems and worries you might face after your relative has moved into a home, but there are many positive ways you can be involved too.

Your continued love and support will help your relative keep her individuality and her contact with the world outside the care home. Regular visits, trips, outings and holidays can help her feel she is still a valued member of your family.

You could also get more involved with the daily life of the care home, for example by making friends with other residents, making a point of talking to them, remembering their birthdays and anniversaries, even taking them out on visits with your relative sometimes. Sometimes families become so involved in the life of the care home that they carry on visiting, and keep up friendships with other residents, even after their relative has died. Or you could help with activities by sharing some of your skills or hobbies with a group of residents, for example gardening, music or crafts.

The Relatives Association (address on p 87) is a national organisation which offers support and advice to families with a relative in a care home, and works to improve standards and build understanding between relatives, residents, home providers and staff.

Doris

'Yes, they're very caring. But do you know what I appreciate most? They give you your freedom.'

'I'm 94, and I've been a widow for 37 years, so I've learnt to manage on my own. I had a lovely bungalow with beautiful views, which I was loath to leave. I thought I was coping well. But after I was knocked down by a car and fractured my femur I couldn't walk too well, and my GP suggested a nursing home. I resisted because I thought I was coping. However, I found just looking after myself, shopping and cooking and keeping the bungalow clean, was making me so tired.

'So I went with my friend to visit a number of homes. As soon as we came to this one, we both said, 'This is it'. I can't put my finger on what it was – it was just the atmosphere. And the garden – the garden looked lovely.

'I put my name down, and within a fortnight they had a vacancy. That was a bit sooner than I'd expected, and it didn't leave me much time to make arrangements. But they were so kind and cooperative. They helped me bring over my own bed and some other furniture. The bed that was in the room went into store. And they stored some of my possessions for me. As soon as I'd put my pictures up on the walls, I felt at home. I went to bed that night and I just felt as if I was at home.

'I thought I might be sad when my bungalow was sold, because I'd lived there 25 years, but I found I didn't mind at all. It was just the ending of things. But I've no regrets now, no nostalgia. I've started a new life.

'I settled in straight away. They're so kind here. Whatever you ask for – it's no problem. I have a lot of visitors, and they always offer a cup of tea. Yes, they're very caring. But do you know what I appreciate most? They give you your freedom.'

Useful addresses

Abbeyfield Society
Housing association specialising in bedsits for older people in shared houses with meals provided.

53 Victoria Street
St Albans
Hertfordshire AR1 3UW
Tel: 01727 857536

Age Concern England
Provides advice, information and services for older people; local groups throughout the country.

1268 London Road
London SW16 4ER
Tel: 0181-679 8000

Alzheimer Scotland – Action on Dementia
Information, support and advice about dementia and 24-hour Helpline for carers and people with dementia living in Scotland.

22 Drumsheugh Gardens
Edinburgh EH3 7RN
Tel: 0131-243 1453
Helpline: 0800 317 817

Alzheimer's Disease Society
Information, support and advice about caring for someone with Alzheimer's disease.

Gordon House
10 Greencoat Place
London SW1P 1PH
Tel: 0171-306 0606

Arthritis Care
Advice about living with arthritis, loan of equipment, holiday centres. Local branches in many areas.

18 Stephenson Way
London NW1 2HD
Tel: 0171-916 1500

Association of Charity Officers
How to find out about charities which could help you (please write first).

Beechwood House
Wyllyotts Close
Potters Bar
Hertfordshire EN6 2HN
Tel: 01707 651777

Association of Crossroads Care Attendant Schemes
See Crossroads Care

British Association for Counselling
To find out about counselling services in your area.

1 Regent Place
Rugby
Warwickshire CV21 2PJ
Tel: 01788 578328/9

British Federation of Care Home Proprietors
Can send a list of homes which are members, and give general advice.

Elmsdale House
Wood Street North
Alfreton
Derbyshire DE55 7GR
Tel: 01773 831966

Calibre
Free cassette library for blind people.

Aylesbury
Buckingham HP22 5XQ
Tel: 01296 432339/81211

Care and Repair
Advice about home repairs and improvements.

Castle House
Kirtley Drive
Nottingham NG7 1LD
Tel: 0115 979 9091

Carers National Association
Information and advice if you are caring for someone. Can put you in touch with other carers and carers' groups in your area.

20–25 Glasshouse Yard
London EC1A 4JS
Tel: 0171-490 8818
(1–4pm weekdays)

Charity Search
Free information about help from charities.

25 Portview Road
Avonmouth
Bristol BS11 9LD
Tel: 0117 982 4060

Chest, Heart and Stroke Scotland (CHSS)
Aims to improve the quality of life for people in Scotland affected by chest, heart or stroke illness through medical research, health promotion, advice and information, and the provision of services.

65 North Castle Street
Edinburgh EH2 3LT
Tel: 0131-225 6963

Citizens Advice Bureau
For advice on legal, financial and consumer matters. A good place to turn to if you don't know where to go for help or advice on any subject.

Listed in local telephone directories, or in the *Yellow Pages* under 'Counselling and advice'. Other local advice centres may also be listed.

Community Health Council
For enquiries or complaints about any aspect of the NHS in your area. (Called Health Councils in Scotland.)

See the local telephone directory for your area (sometimes listed under Health Authority).

Continence Foundation
Advice and information about whom to contact with incontinence problems.

The Basement
2 Doughty Street
London WC1N 2PH
Tel: 0171-404 6875

Counsel and Care
Advice for elderly people and their families; can sometimes give grants to help people remain at home or return to their home.

Lower Ground Floor
Twyman House
16 Bonny Street
London NW1 9PG
Tel: 0171-485 1566
(10am–4pm)

Court of Protection
If you need to take over the affairs of someone who is mentally incapable (in England and Wales).

Public Trust Office
Protection Division
Stewart House
24 Kingsway
London WC2B 6JX
Tel: 0171-664 7300

Crossroads Care
For a care attendant to come and look after your relative at home.

10 Regent Place
Rugby
Warwickshire CV21 2PN
Tel: 01788 573653

Disabled Living Centres Council
Can tell you your nearest disabled living centre, where you can see and try out aids and equipment.

1st Floor
Winchester House
11 Cranmer Road
London SW9 6EJ
Tel: 0171-820 0567

Disabled Living Foundation
Information about aids to help you cope with a disability.

380–384 Harrow Road
London W9 2HU
Tel: 0171-289 6111
Helpline: 0870 603 9177

Elderly Accommodation Counsel
Computerised information about private and voluntary accommodation for older people, by area and/or price range.

46a Chiswick High Road
London W4 1SZ
Tel: 0181-995 8320/
742 1182

Holiday Care Service
Free information and advice about holidays for elderly or disabled people and their carers.

2nd Floor
Imperial Buildings
Victoria Road
Horley
Surrey RH6 7PZ
Tel: 01293 774535

Incontinence Information Helpline

Tel: 0191-213 0050
(9am–6pm Mon–Fri)

Independent Healthcare Association
Representative and lobbying organisation for private care homes.

22 Little Russell Street
London WC1A 2HT
Tel: 0171-430 0537

Jewish Care
Social care, personal support, residential homes for Jewish people.

Stuart Young House
221 Golders Green Road
London NW11 9DQ
Tel: 0181-458 3282/
922 2123

John Groom's Association for Disabled People
Residential, respite and holiday accommodation.

50 Scrutton Street
London EC2A 4PH
Tel: 0171-452 2000

Leonard Cheshire Foundation
Residential homes and home care attendants mainly but not exclusively for younger disabled people.

26–29 Maunsel Street
London SW1P 2QN
Tel: 0171-828 1822

Local Government Ombudsman
Looks into complaints about maladministration by local authorities that cause injustice.

21 Queen Anne's Gate
London SW1H 9BU
Tel: 0171-915 3210

MIND (National Association for Mental Health)
Information, support and publications about all aspects of mental illness, depression, etc.

Granta House
15–19 Broadway
Stratford
London E15 4BQ
Tel: 0181-519 2122

National Care Homes Association
An umbrella body for local associations of private care homes; can put you in touch with homes in your area, and give you advice.

Martin House
3rd Floor
84–86 Gray's Inn Road
London WC1X 8BQ
Tel: 0171-831 7090

Parkinson's Disease Society
Information and advice for people caring for someone with Parkinson's disease; many local branches.

22 Upper Woburn Place
London WC1H 0RA
Tel: 0171-383 3513

Partially Sighted Society
Advice, information and aids for partially sighted people.

Low Vision Advice Service
PO Box 322
Doncaster DN1 2XA
Tel: 01302 323132

Registered Nursing Home Association
Information about registered nursing homes in your area.

Calthorpe House
Hagley Road
Edgbaston
Birmingham B16 8QY
Tel: 0121-454 2511

Relatives Association
Support and advice for the relatives of people in a residential or nursing home or in a hospital long-term.

5 Tavistock Place
London WC1H 9SS
Tel: 0171-916 6055/
0181-201 9153

Royal National Institute for Deaf People (RNID)
Information and advice about all aspects of hearing loss; information about hearing aids.

19–23 Featherstone Street
London EC1Y 8SL
Tel: 0171-296 8000
(Voice)

Royal National Institute for the Blind (RNIB)
Information and advice for blind people and their families.

224 Great Portland Street
London WIN 6AA
Tel: 0171-388 1266

Samaritans
Someone to talk to if you are in despair.

See your local telephone directory.

Shaftesbury Society
Sheltered housing for elderly people.

16–20 Kingston Road
London SW19 1JZ
Tel: 0181-239 5555

Soldiers, Sailors and Airmen Family Association (SSAFA)
Help for service or ex-service men and women and their families.

19 Queen Elizabeth Street
London SE1 2LP
Tel: 0171-403 8783

Standing Conference of Ethnic Minority Senior Citizens
Information, support and advice for older people from ethnic minorities and their families.

5 Westminster Bridge Road
London SE1 7XW
Tel: 0171-928 0095

Stroke Association
Information and advice if you have had a stroke or are caring for someone who has had one.

123–127 Whitecross Street
London EC1Y 8JJ
Tel: 0171-490 7999

Sue Ryder Foundation
Homes for disabled people.

Sue Ryder Homes
Cavendish
Sudbury
Suffolk CO10 8AY
Tel: 01787 280252

Talking Newspaper Association of the United Kingdom
Talking newspapers for blind and short-sighted people.

National Recording Centre
Heathfield
East Sussex TN21 8DB
Tel: 01435 866102

United Kingdom Home Care Association
For information about organisations providing home care in your area.

42 Banstead Road
Carshalton Beeches
Surrey SM5 3NW
Tel: 0181-288 1551

About Age Concern

Finding and paying for residential and nursing home care is one of a wide range of publications produced by Age Concern England, the National Council on Ageing. Age Concern cares about all older people and believes later life should be fulfilling and enjoyable. For too many this is impossible. As the leading charitable movement in the UK concerned with ageing and older people, Age Concern finds effective ways to change that situation.

Where possible, we enable older people to solve problems themselves, providing as much or as little support as they need. Our network of 1,400 local groups, supported by 250,000 volunteers, provides community-based services such as lunch clubs, day centres and home visiting.

Nationally, we take a lead role in campaigning, parliamentary work, policy analysis, research, specialist information and advice provision, and publishing. Innovative programmes promote healthier lifestyles and provide older people with opportunities to give the experience of a lifetime back to their communities.

Age Concern is dependent on donations, covenants and legacies.

Age Concern England
1268 London Road
London SW16 4ER
Tel: 0181-679 8000

Age Concern Scotland
113 Rose Street
Edinburgh EH2 3DT
Tel: 0131-220 3345

Age Concern Cymru
4th Floor
1 Cathedral Road
Cardiff CF1 9SD
Tel: 01222 371566

Age Concern Northern Ireland
3 Lower Crescent
Belfast BT7 1NR
Tel: 01232 245729

Other books in this series

The Carer's Handbook: What to do and who to turn to
Marina Lewycka
At some point in their lives millions of people find themselves suddenly responsible for organising the care of an older person with a health crisis. All too often such carers have no idea what services are available or who can be approached for support. This book is designed to act as a first point of reference in just such an emergency, signposting readers on to many more detailed, local sources of advice.
£6.99 0–86242–262–0

Caring for someone who is dying
Penny Mares
Confronting the knowledge that a loved one is going to die soon is always a moment of crisis. And the pain of the news can be compounded by the need to take responsibility for the care and support given in the last months and weeks. This book attempts to help readers cope with their emotions and make all the necessary practical arrangements.
£6.99 0–86242–260–4

Publications from Age Concern Books

Health and care

The Community Care Handbook: The reformed system explained (2nd edition)
Barbara Meredith
Written by one of the country's leading experts, the new edition of this hugely successful handbook provides a comprehensive overview of the first two years of implementation of the community care reforms and examines how the system has evolved.

£13.99 0-86242-171-3

Money matters

Your Rights: A guide to money benefits for older people
Sally West
A highly acclaimed annual guide to the State benefits available to older people. Contains current information on Income Support, Housing Benefit, Council Tax Benefit and Retirement Pensions, among other sources of financial help, and includes advice on how to claim them.

For further information, please telephone 0181-679 8000.

Managing Other People's Money (2nd edition)
Penny Letts
Foreword by the Master of the Court of Protection

The management of money and property is usually a personal and private matter. However, there may come a time when someone else has to take over on either a temporary or a permanent basis. This book looks at the circumstances in which such a need could arise and provides a step-by-step guide to the arrangements which have to be made.

£9.99 0–86242–250–7

Housing

A Buyer's Guide to Retirement Housing

Co-published with the National Housing and Town Planning Council

This book is designed to answer many of the questions older people may have when looking to buy a flat or bungalow in a sheltered scheme. In clear and straightforward language, it provides comprehensive information for older people, their families and friends, including topics such as:

- the pros and cons;
- the design and management of schemes;
- the charges and costs;
- what to look for when comparing units.

Detailed advice is also provided on areas such as the running costs, location and terms of ownership. This popular book – now in its 3rd edition – will provide all the information needed to make an informed decision.

£4.95 0–86242–127–6

If you would like to order any of these titles, please write to the address below, enclosing a cheque or money order for the appropriate amount made payable to Age Concern England. Credit card orders may be made on 0181-679 8000.

Mail Order Unit
Age Concern England
1268 London Road
London SW16 4ER

Factsheets from Age Concern

Covering many areas of concern to older people, Age Concern's factsheets are comprehensive and totally up to date. There are over 40 factsheets, with each one providing straightforward information and impartial advice in a simple and easy-to-use format. Topics covered include:

- finding and paying for residential and nursing home care
- raising income from your home
- money benefits
- legal arrangements for managing financial affairs
- finding help at home

Single copies are available free on receipt of a 9" × 12" sae.

Age Concern offers a factsheet subscription service which presents all the factsheets in a folder, together with regular updates throughout the year. The first year's subscription currently costs £40; an annual renewal thereafter is £20.

> For further information, or to order factsheets, write to:
>
> **Information and Policy Division**
> Age Concern England
> 1268 London Road
> London SW16 4ER

For readers in Scotland wishing further information, or to order factsheets, please write to:

Age Concern Scotland
113 Rose Street
Edinburgh EH2 3DT

Subscribers in Scotland will automatically be sent Scottish editions of factsheets where law and practice differ in Scotland.

Index